The Hidden Force Within

Practical Tools to Integrate Energy Medicine into Your Health and Healing

Sarah Lascano

The Hidden Force Within
by Sarah Lascano

Published by Legacy Press Books
A subsidiary of S & P Productions, Inc.
311 Main Street, Suite D
El Segundo, CA 90245
310-640-8885
www.legacypressbooks.com

Published and Printed in the United States of America

ISBN: 978-0-9996519-4-0

Disclaimer

The information in this book is for educational purposes only. Nothing is intended for or should be taken as medical advice or treatment. Energy healing is not a substitute for care by your therapist or doctor. Please direct any questions regarding your care to your healthcare professionals.

DEDICATION

This book is dedicated to my mother, Josephine Citrin, who taught me to be a thought leader and inspired me to support those who yearn for spiritual and energetic healing during their difficult health journeys.

Table of Contents

Foreword

It was the dreaded appointment day, my second appointment with the oncologist. The diagnosis was bleak: stage 4 pancreatic cancer metastasized to the lungs. The doctor provided one treatment option: an every-other-week chemotherapy regimen that would extend median life expectancy from two months without treatment to 11 to 12 months with treatment. During the seven months before this appointment, I had undergone testing, referrals, bloodwork, scans and biopsies, all with too much poking, prodding, waiting and stressing.

Five weeks prior to that dreaded appointment, I began working with Sarah Lascano, an energy medicine practitioner. I clearly recall our first phone conversation. Sarah listened as I shared my story. She asked me what I wanted to gain by meeting with her. I articulated as best I could that I wanted to feel more balanced as I faced the future.

She listened and said, "What about feeling better?" I was taken aback by this question! I was stunned, surprised, intrigued and for the first time in months felt hope. I managed to say, "I hadn't thought about it but I would love to feel better." And just like that, Sarah and I began our journey.

My first appointment with Sarah began with us getting to know one another. I had filled out a brief questionnaire on general health, family history, childhood memories and recent emotions I experienced. We discussed questionnaire information along with nutrition and vitamins. Given the choice of remaining seated or lying on her examination table for our session, I chose her table and Sarah sat beside me.

I was nervous as Sarah gently touched my wrist to read my energy and began sharing what she was sensing. I was astounded when she began to tell me things about myself that were true that I hadn't shared. While I didn't confirm or deny these things, I was wondering what powers this woman possessed that she knew those things.

At this first appointment, I learned I have an innate ability to heal my body. In fact, everyone does. I learned that we would use energy healing to move blocks from my body and then we would work on strengthening my immune system. Sarah wrote two affirmations on note paper and I left with instructions to place the paper where I would see it: "I am open to receive," and "I am protected, supported, guided, led." When I left her office, I felt lighter, hopeful and more like myself than I had in months.

As I worked with Sarah, I learned about her own journey to become an energy medicine practitioner, how she developed and uses her unique method of practicing energy healing and how she guides her clients to move and cleanse their own energy. Sarah found her calling to energy medicine because of her own health crisis 19 years earlier. Not finding solutions within Western medicine, Sarah applied the same rigorous scientific research principles she developed as a daughter who grew up working in her father's surgical clinic and as a nursing assistant at the local hospital. Her engineering training also served her well when she turned to the world of holistic medicine on her quest to recover her health and that of her child.

As Sarah increased her knowledge and skills using various types of holistic medicine, she developed her own unique approach to healing with energy medicine. Sarah is an intuitive energy healer. She has the ability to read the body and combine this information with focused energy medicine techniques. Thus, each session is unique, providing what is needed to cleanse the client's energy and gently move them forward. The entire person is addressed as Sarah helps integrate one's physical, emotional, mental and spiritual bodies.

Through her healing sessions, Sarah empowers clients to work with their own energy. They learn tools for working with challenging emotions, gently moving blocked or stuck energy and improving their mindset. This leaves them feeling empowered to effect change in themselves. Hence, the title Sarah chose for this book is *The Hidden Force Within: Practical Tools to Integrate Energy Medicine into Your Health and*

Healing is apropos. The book explains the basics of energy followed by the process she uses with her clients to allow energy to heal the body, mind and spirit.

When I returned to the oncologist for the dreaded appointment, I listened politely to the official diagnosis of my disease, the treatment options and prognosis. Then the doctor politely listened as I thanked him for giving me the information I needed to make an informed decision and answering our family's questions.

I shared my feeling that I wouldn't be the patient he described based on statistics. I respectfully declined traditional treatment and stated I would continue my holistic practices. The doctor said he wasn't surprised, noticing that I had gained weight since our first appointment and was the healthiest-looking pancreatic cancer patient he had ever encountered.

Each energy session with Sarah was unique. In the beginning, our sessions focused on removing energy blocks caused primarily by fear but other emotions too, such as anxiety and grief. Sarah discerned the blockages in various parts of my body. Removing them seemed to occur in layers.

In between our sessions, I did my own energy work. I had access to Elevate, Sarah's digital healing sessions. The in-person and digital sessions helped tremendously to alleviate and get rid of anxiety and fear. I learned Sarah's process to recognize negative emotion, acknowledge it and then ask it to leave my body. I learned that the mind is powerful, as is the importance of envisioning what you want and how you want to feel. Journaling became a new outlet for me.

Over time, our sessions gradually focused on my cancer. We used energy to boost my immune system to allow my cells to become more robust, with an improved ability to identify cancerous cells and subsume them. Sometimes we would imagine white light bringing healing to my body and comfort to my mind.

Due to my work with Sarah, I understand the role positive thoughts, emotions and affirmations play in healing, the importance of moving energy blockages and the use of energy medicine to boost my immune system and destroy diseased cells. Energy medicine concepts allowed me to integrate my spiritual, mental, emotional and physical bodies to discover the authentic me. I am thankful to have been reintroduced to the hidden force in me that allowed me to return to wholeness and live longer than any of my doctors thought possible.

If you are seeking answers regarding your health, I recommend Sarah's book. It is readable, understandable and most importantly, it can immediately allow you to begin healing. My advice to you, the reader, is to be open to receive and you will be supported, guided and led.

Cindia Stewart

Author's note: Cindia's decision not to seek medical treatment was a personal decision made with her family. She went on to live almost a full year with a high quality of life with Stage IV pancreatic cancer, spending precious moments with her family and even teaching her beloved yoga classes. She exceeded her oncologist's life expectancy by five times with a high quality of life, as was her wish.

Introduction: How Did I Get Here?

Perhaps you have health symptoms that aren't responding to treatment. Maybe you've been told there is nothing else that can be done to help you. Or maybe you desire a healthy body that ages with grace and ease. Whatever brought you here, I'm excited to share the invisible factors that contribute to symptoms, teach simple tools you can use to improve your health and provide expert healing you can use right now to feel better.

My passion is simple: to empower your health. I wish I had known about this invisible force when my health crashed. Years ago, I was pregnant with my first child when I had a nasty bout of food poisoning. Two weeks later, I developed eczema, joint pain, low energy and digestive woes. I hoped this would all disappear with the baby's arrival, but a few months postpartum, the symptoms continued to worsen.

I began my quest for answers. Doctors had nothing to offer except to avoid foods that caused symptoms. Since I was sensitive to 80% of what I ate, that option didn't feel sustainable. The engineer in me knew there had to be a way to unwind what had happened when my health began a downward spiral. After years of researching and trying healing diets, naturopaths, integrative doctors, herbalists and more, I was on the verge of giving up hope. I feared I'd never be able to reclaim my health when I finally found the missing piece of my health puzzle: energy medicine and the mind-body-energy connection.

After just a few energy medicine sessions, I suddenly made miraculous progress. As you will learn, you too have the power to change what is happening in your body with highly effective noninvasive means, healing symptoms as big as chronic pain, cancer, infections and debilitating anxiety. It's my passion to cut years off your healing journey by sharing what I've learned as a patient and now as a practitioner who has helped hundreds of people heal their hard-to-treat symptoms.

Your body is an amazing machine, programmed at the cellular level to constantly move toward health and well-being. The body has an innate ability to heal. If this is true, how did you get to a place where it doesn't feel well no matter how hard you try? The problem is easier to understand if you look at the body as a whole system, not just as a physical body. Your body is more than just organs and tissues; it's also thoughts, emotions, soul and energy. Health relies on communication and the unhindered flow of energy between all parts of your system.

The human body has a wide variety of repair and protection mechanisms. Did you know most people have genetically damaged cells that could lead to cancer throughout their lifetime? It's true, but the body has mechanisms to prevent disease. The immune system searches, cleans and repairs. In the case of health symptoms, we must ask what happened in your body that allowed the usual protection and repair mechanisms to fail. Rest assured, you can recover your body's ability to heal and I will share how in the coming chapters. As your ability to heal is repaired, untreatable symptoms can suddenly improve or even disappear, pain recedes and infections clear. The results can be nothing short of miraculous.

A Healthcare Paradigm Shift

To achieve healing that feels impossible, we need a paradigm shift in how we think about healthcare. Our Western health system focuses on symptoms and remedies: medicines, therapies, surgeries. This works beautifully for acute illness and injuries. If you have appendicitis, a broken bone or a head injury, this approach to care is exactly what you need.

Chronic symptoms on the other hand require a different approach. Diabetes, chronic pain, anxiety disorders, digestive problems and chronic infections require looking deeper to find what is blocking the body, preventing healing. Focusing on symptoms is only a Band-Aid approach. The problem resurfaces or the symptoms come back unless we identify the root cause of dysfunction. This requires a shift in how we view healing and medical treatment. What imbalance in the body allowed symptoms to appear? In the coming chapters, I discuss exactly how to discover and address these imbalances.

When we delve deeper, we find that any kind of stress can affect the body's function and result in symptoms. The symptoms don't have to be related to the cause, though they can be. A stomach ulcer results from too much stomach acid, but what causes too much stomach acid? Out-of-balance bacteria can cause such symptoms, but why are they overgrown in the first place? If we hope to heal the ulcer and prevent recurrence, we must identify and address the energetic component: worry, anxiety or other energy that found its way into the stomach.

The first step toward healing is to stop accumulating and storing emotional and physical stress. This happens when energy exceeds your ability to cope. Perhaps you felt unsafe, ridiculed or shamed for expressing emotion or perhaps you lacked skills or support to process how you were feeling. When emotional energy is bigger than you can handle, it is stored instead of being expressed and felt. When you choose a different pattern and constructively process this energy, a wonderful thing happens. The current emotional stress is processed, and past energy locked in the body releases. In the stomach ulcer example, stomach acid production will return to normal levels, ulcers resolve and symptoms disappear, healing the root cause. This is possible for big symptoms like cancer, tick infections, chronic pain, bowel disease and more.

The body's energy system includes the body, mind and soul. With energy healing, we work with all these parts at once to heal the body from the foundation. In my practice, the root cause of illness is usually not related to symptoms. By focusing on strengthening the body from the ground up, we release blockages that hamper the immune system, slow digestion and keep the nervous system in fight-or-flight mode. This process allows the body to take a giant exhale, relax at the cellular level and get to work healing in a way that lasts.

So how did illness or imbalance begin? Stress disrupts the body's energy. In modern life, we often don't set aside time to recover from stress. We jump into the workday, move on to the next tight deadline or fail to get restorative rest. Lack of valuable recovery time allows no opportunity for the body to repair. If ongoing stress continues to accumulate, the system will be on the edge of collapse and another major event can easily trigger a major health crash.

For me, it was a bout of food poisoning that sent my body and gut into a tailspin of chronic inflammation. For others, divorce, a car accident or infection can all be triggers. One significant stress can cause the house of cards to collapse and tumble into illness.

But there is a way to unwind the past, repair the body and strengthen the future. Let's dive in.

Note: Before you keep reading, please turn to Appendix A to complete a short questionnaire. Please don't skip this step! This questionnaire allows you to note how you feel before completing the exercises in this book. After the healing session, you'll have the opportunity to revisit the evaluation to note any changes.

Part I. Meet Your Mind-Body Energy System

Chapter 1: Your Miraculous Machine

Case Study: Bacterial Infections

Lisa came for help with anxiety that was controlling her life. She had no energy and could barely function because of chronic pain and anxiety. Her two elementary-age children were homeschooled due to anxiety and health issues; they had been at home all year, unable to go to school. The children struggled mentally and physically, having major anxiety and panic attacks if Lisa left the house. The daughter had severe separation anxiety and the son could not regulate his emotions, resulting in terrifying rages.

The children had been diagnosed with PANDAS (Pediatric Autoimmune Neuropsychiatric Disorders Associated with Streptococcal Infections) and were treated by multiple doctors without progress. They completed a multiple-month antibiotic regimen prescribed by a specialist, tried months of holistic care with supplements, herbs and integrative therapies, yet their antibody levels didn't improve. Lisa was out of ideas when their request for help came across my desk.

In our work together, we released energy around Lisa's difficult childhood, including her parents' divorce, an emotionally abusive stepmother and parents who seemed to regard children as an inconvenience. Healing focused deeply on rebuilding mom's immune system in the gut, spleen, and thymus gland, and boundaries with her parents, partner and children. She began to prioritize her own health, which she struggled to balance with her children's special needs. Emotional energies of not feeling safe or wanted due to Lisa's unsettled childhood and feeling unsupported by her partner cleared from her system.

Within eight months of working with Lisa and her children, the results were stunning. The children were back in school and thriving, earning As and Bs without medication. Mom was able to discontinue 14 different daily medications, including anti-anxiety, sleep aids, antidepressants, fibromyalgia medication and pain pills. Before, she couldn't climb stairs or walk around the block due to her pain levels. Now, she was free from all these symptoms.

✑

When you think about your body, you are likely thinking of your hands, belly, head and other body parts. You may consider what your body does for you: digest food, walk through the grocery store, breathe, circulate blood. Did you know this is just part of the story? In addition to all this physical wonder, also included are the parts you can't see, such as your mind and energy.

The parts you can't see impact your health just as much as the parts you can see. Research proves that emotions and thoughts impact physical function. A variety of stresses change your body's physical chemistry and levels of stress chemicals. In fact, research shows that your intestinal microbiome changes its function based on how you feel[1].

If we know the mind is so influential to health, why isn't it addressed as part of routine medical care? Research abounds proving the link between disease and stress[2]. The mind and body are intimately connected. Both must be addressed to create a thriving resilient body and mind. This is even more influential when treating chronic health conditions. By taking the whole system into account, the untreatable can be treated and the unhealable a thing of the past.

The body is a beautifully engineered machine, governed by innate intelligence that supports it through life and knows how to heal. It's awe inspiring when you consider the entire body starts from just two cells and results in differentiated organs, systems and even your personality. The intricate timing of puberty, menopause and other major life changes happens without direction or prompt. When you cut your finger, your body jumps to work immediately, without prompting from the mind. Immune cells jump into action, circulation increases and the body halts bleeding, fights infection, closes the wound and begins healing. It's nothing short of miraculous.

An amazing coordination of processes happens daily, intricately woven together to keep you safe. The most profound fact is that the conscious mind isn't involved. This intelligence exists naturally in all of us, without training or intervention from the mind, keeping the body functioning smoothly.

The Body as a System

Systems theory tells us that a system is more than the sum of its parts. The body's system consists of the physical body, mind, emotions, soul and energy. Addressing only one part may bring temporary relief, but other parts of the system may get neglected, especially if your symptoms are chronic or degenerative in nature.

> **Fundamental principle:** The body is a system composed of mind, body and spirit. A change in one part of the system affects the entire system.

Typically, current healthcare efforts address only the physical body even though the interrelationships, dependencies and connections between all parts of you affect the function of your entire system. All of you must be considered holistically to recover health long-term. Sure, you can treat individual symptoms like indigestion or an achy joint with medication or treat an infection with success, but consider this: why is the symptom there in the first place? What imbalance in the body led to that symptom? Imbalances are the root cause of illness and must be addressed for long-lasting relief and health.

Not only does addressing the full body system lead to longer-lasting healing, this integrative approach also heals symptoms that don't respond to other treatments. Some people whose conditions persist may be told that their health problems are all in their heads and prescribed anxiety medication. When medical options are exhausted, others hear there's nothing else to be done. Either case leaves patients feeling out of options and hopeless.

But there is hope. I've seen energy medicine create space for the human body to access its innate ability to heal, allowing recovery from what might have seemed untreatable. Research, including the work of S. Jain and R. Hammerschlag, documents the success of mind-body energy-healing techniques[3].

What I share in this book is backed by research. Put this knowledge to work for you to heal imbalances and boost your health and resilience. Not only will you stay healthier, but you'll also be empowered with the knowledge that symptoms can be healed when you consider the entire system.

How the Body Communicates

Do you think of your body as simply a massive clump of cells without intelligence? If you're frustrated with how it feels or functions, you may view it as a liability instead of a supportive force.

Innate intelligence exists, even though at times it becomes blocked and malfunctions. (More on this soon!) Not only does it exist, but it also has specific ways of communicating with you. Since the body can't talk to you with words, it uses less explicit ways of sharing information. The two primary methods we will discuss here are **symptoms** and **intuition**.

> **Fundamental principle:** Symptoms are the body's way of communicating with you. The body can't use words; it uses symptoms to notify you that something needs to change.

You may think of a symptom as something unpleasant that needs to be fixed. But did you ever consider that your body may be trying to tell you something? In my experience, a symptom tries to get your attention, begging you to take notice, and asking for a change. Your body can't use words to speak to you, so instead it generates feelings, sensations and yes, even dysfunction.

When you feel discomfort, pause for a moment to ask yourself what those symptoms might be telling you. They can share clues to the next steps that might help symptoms to resolve. In the coming chapters, I'll show you exactly how to do this.

> **Fundamental principle:** Intuition allows the body to communicate with you—without the discomfort of symptoms.

Intuition is the other way the body communicates with you. You may think that following intuition is something for other people, but we all have access to this inner wisdom. Consider everyday occurrences. Have you ever left your house and, as you drove away, suddenly remembered you forgot something? Have you ever focused on a problem, unsure of your next step and you "just happen" to see an acquaintance who shares a perfect solution? Have you thought of a family member out of the blue, only to have them call you a short time later?

Those are moments of intuition. Sudden inspiration, remembering, receiving sudden clarity about a problem—those are all ways your intuition speaks to you. I call this "everyday intuition," an amazingly powerful force. Yes, you have it even if you don't realize it; we all do. Once you discover its communication, you can nurture it, boosting your body's ability to talk, guide and support you. There are a variety of ways to tap into this intelligence and use it to guide you forward.

In the coming chapters, we will discuss exactly how to learn to listen to this part of you so it can share important information on how to heal symptoms that may be dragging you down.

The Impact of Stress

Your body is incredibly resilient, but there's a limit to how much stress it can tolerate before health is affected. Your body has resources and mechanisms to keep going, even when the going gets tough. Stress is seemingly unavoidable in modern life and takes a toll on the body. Even "good" stress like a holiday gathering or family wedding celebration can negatively affect you.

At first, stress isn't a big deal. An occasional late night, a bout of illness, a difficult breakup—these are everyday occurrences you can usually recover from in just a few days. But stress in life is not isolated. In fact, often one stress piles upon another. The world doesn't stop just because your child was sick all night and you only got a few hours of sleep. When there's no recovery time before the next major stressor, it's harder for the body to keep going without experiencing negative effects.

Stress is normal, but it's not healthy. Over time, it burdens and disturbs your body's ability to heal. Your body's innate intelligence is still there like a trusted friend, but static starts to build, blocking its ability to communicate and correct imbalances. Mental, emotional, or physical stresses start to drain your healing reserves.

Physical stress like lack of sleep, infection, injury or poor diet is straightforward. Emotional stress can be obvious or less evident. Examples of emotional stressors include losing a loved one, a relationship breakup or anxiety. Less obvious sources of emotional stress—like work stress, fear of making mistakes or not feeling accepted—disturb your body's balance. Spiritual stressors include destructive relationships, codependency or power imbalances. As these stresses burden your body, it's harder to sleep, you may suffer digestive problems and other chronic symptoms of stress begin to accumulate.

Just look to your nervous system for an example of this domino effect: a work or school deadline has you working late hours for a couple of weeks. You don't get enough sleep and your diet suffers. You cut corners and eat more convenience foods. You make your deadline, but your body has accumulated a lot of stress. When you finally have time to sit down and rest, your body feels "wired but tired," and deep sleep is nowhere to be found.

Unless you find a way to deeply restore your energy reserves, your body sets the stage for illness. How? A downhill cycle of less resilience and inefficiency begins unless you take time for extra rest to allow your body to catch up. Your hormonal system and nervous system get locked in "fight-or-flight" mode. In fight-or-flight, your body produces adrenaline and cortisol, stress hormones that take your body out of balanced operation mode and into danger mode. Digestion is shunted, the immune system is off-balance and metabolism and the cardiovascular system shift focus. Your entire body feels the effects as you try to outrun the proverbial tiger. If this were just an isolated event, your body would gradually recover mental and physical balance. But in the typical modern lifestyle, the next stress is not far away. Too often restorative downtime doesn't happen. The body experiences stress after stress, which becomes the new normal.

If the body knows how to heal and stress disrupts this healing capability, illness is the result of the body being disconnected from its innate ability to heal. Simple logic says if you recover this innate intelligence, you can recover your body's ability to heal. Even though you can't see it, the body's energy system is a highly effective tool to release the impact of past stress and reclaim your health. I'm going to show you just how you can recover your body's innate intelligence. But first, let's dive into the hidden force that governs the foundation of your health.

Chapter 2: The Hidden Force Driving Your Health

If you've ever spent time in a hospital, you've likely seen an electrocardiogram machine (EKG). Doctors have been using this machine since its invention by Willem Einthoven in 1895. Fun fact: Einthoven won the Nobel Prize in 1924 for the EKG. Suffice it to say, after more than one hundred years, modern medicine is comfortable with the heart's energy system and the electrical impulses that govern heart rhythm.

Modern medicine recognizes the energy system of the brain and nervous system: doctors use the electroencephalograph machine (EEG) to measure the brain's electrical system. Invented in 1924 by Hans Berger, today it records brain activity (energy waves). Doctors use nerve conduction studies to measure electrical impulses traveling through nerves in different parts of the body. This process is like examining the wiring in your home. EKG, EEG and nerve conduction studies measure energy in the body.

Although these scientific measuring tools have been around for 100 years, acupuncturists and other healers have known for centuries that subtle energy exists throughout the human body, not just the heart, brain and nerves. Energy healing uses this subtle energy, as do other modalities, including acupuncture, Reiki and Quantum Touch. The heart and brain are the body's strongest energy fields, easily measured by EKG and EEG. Even though the subtle energy system found in other areas of the body is not as easily quantified, it is extensive and influences the entire body.

The energy system is designed like the electrical system in a house. Energy comes into the system and travels down pathways, much like circuits. Nerves, meridians and energy centers provide a vast network for energy to circulate throughout the body, affecting organs, glands, and tissues, helping digestion function as intended, moving muscles as desired and even sensing a hot stove to move quickly away to prevent injury.

Without these nerve and energy highways and the electrical impulses that travel along them, your muscles and organs would not work. Energy makes everything possible.

Case Study: Surgery Recovery

Allen did not look forward to back surgery. He had significant pain for years and had tried steroid injections to avoid the spinal surgery recommended for him. As a retired physician, he knew it would not be easy to recover from surgery, but with his pain increasing and other options exhausted, he scheduled the procedure.

It was completed without complications and recovery seemed textbook, even better given his high tolerance for pain. He exceeded recovery goals in physical therapy and took fewer doses of pain medications than prescribed.

The only issue was his sense of taste: all foods tasted revolting. Coffee, usually a beloved staple of his morning routine, tasted too awful to drink. Eggs tasted rotten; meat tasted spoiled. He hoped this side effect would resolve on its own, but in the three weeks following surgery, he lost 25 pounds. With his medical training, he knew a lack of protein would impede his recovery. His body needed nutrition to heal bone, repair skin and strengthen muscles. He had no idea how to resolve the situation that appeared as soon as he awoke from surgery.

I did an energy healing session for him to shift out energy blockages caused by surgical trauma. I cleared the physical sensations of pain and helplessness during his surgery recovery and the need to rely on others for basic needs. I disconnected the emotional trauma and physical pain from any association with eating eggs or feeling powerless during recovery. The very next day, his sense of taste had largely reverted to normal. He was able to eat eggs! The results were impressive; however, he still couldn't tolerate the taste of coffee.

The following day, I cleared the physical and emotional pain related to all foods. After this second session, he could taste all food normally, including coffee. He proceeded to make a full recovery without further taste anomalies, weight loss or complications.

❧

The Law of Conservation of Energy

While you don't need to learn quantum physics, the law of conservation of energy is important to your health. Chances are good you learned about this law in science class. It states that energy is not created or destroyed, but only changes state. In other words, energy is converted from one form to another, but not destroyed. This is important for your health. If energy isn't released, it is stored in the body. It can't simply vanish; it needs an exit route or it will remain. When you feel an emotion, two primary paths are possible: feel and express it or store it.

Let's say you have a stressful morning—your kids don't listen, your breakfast burns or your refrigerator suddenly stops working. You're aggravated and overwhelmed as you drive to work, struggling to maintain control of your emotions and not explode.

When you arrive at work, all that emotion has to be shelved, so to speak, to get through the day. By the time you get home, you're just irritated and tired. You may have forgotten about the source of the morning's frustrations, but your body is still holding on to the emotional energy because you haven't taken the time to somehow process it. As such, this energy has the potential to be stored in the body where it will begin to block function.

You will learn more about blockages in the next chapter. For now, realize that unprocessed emotional energy can become stored in the body, causing energy blockages that affect your health, both body and mind.

Your Environment Matters

From experience, you know that what's inside you influences how you feel. Lifestyle factors such as sleep, food and stress matter. You probably understand that you don't feel well after a disrupted night of sleep or one too many trips to the taco buffet. What may be harder to grasp is the strong influence on your health from factors outside your body.

Outside influences affect you physically, emotionally and energetically. Have you ever walked into the middle of a heated discussion, only to find yourself suddenly tense? The room energy changes how you feel, impacting your emotions and your body. As you become more tense, your body chemistry shifts, muscles become tight, circulation changes and your nervous system moves into danger mode (fight-or-flight).

Outside factors are environmental influences that affect how you feel. You may have felt the serenity of a wellness spa, the satisfaction of a tidy house or the joy of a surprise birthday party. The energy of a place can drag you down or lift you up. This is not just how you feel; it's the health of your energy, mind and body. Physical variables like heat, humidity, wind and cold matter. You can even be affected by the energy of a location, such as a cancer treatment center or a chaotic preschool.

While environment affects everyone, you have mechanisms to protect your energy from outside influences. Energetic boundaries act as gatekeepers and buffers to protect you from energies in your environment. The strength of your boundaries are affected by your past, your health and your stress levels. When you feel the vibe of a place, you pick up on the energy around you. Sensitivity is governed by the health of your system and how resilient it is to stress, dictating what you notice and how deeply you're affected. Your energetic boundaries act as intelligent gatekeepers, deciding what to allow in and what to deny.

Boundaries allow your system to be unaffected and nonreactive to the environment, protecting you from manipulative or dysregulated people, emotional energy, physical factors and even illness. There are ways to strengthen energetic boundaries to protect yourself from outside factors in the environment, as we will discuss in later chapters. In the next chapter, you will learn what happens energetically when stress of any kind breaches your energetic boundaries, affecting your body. But first, let's define an energy block and explore common causes.

Energy Block Basics

Your body relies on blood circulating freely through it to bring oxygen to every part of you. The energy in your body is similar. The free flow of energy must be maintained for you to be healthy. You have all sorts of energy highways, channels and centers in your body. If there's a major backup, surrounding areas will soon experience traffic gridlock, just like a highway running through a city. Flowing energy is imperative to a balanced healthy system.

If you know what causes energy blockages, you are empowered to take ownership of your health and prevent disruptions in the first place. What causes an energy blockage strong enough to affect your health? Stress of any kind that exceeds your ability to process can disrupt both body and energy.

> **Fundamental principle:** Stress in any form can create energy blockages, impacting your health.

Perhaps you think of stress as a feeling of overwhelm. This is certainly true, but let's broaden the definition of stress by looking at four categories in detail: physical, emotional, mental and spiritual stress.

Physical stress is easy to recognize; you have likely felt its impact. Stress that directly affects the body can include accidents, injuries, infections and hospitalizations. This could be an Epstein-Barr infection (mononucleosis) with a difficult recovery, food poisoning with strong symptoms or a significant injury with lasting effects.

These events may seem to be just part of everyday life, but if you reflect on how you felt both before and after these significant stressors, you may realize you "never felt the same" since your recovery. In fact, accidents and infections may create chronic stress below the radar with no obvious symptoms. This unknowingly distracts your immune system, draining your vitality. In my practice, low grade, chronic infections without obvious symptoms play a major role in chronic illness.

There are also simple stressors that can affect your energy health, especially if they become chronic. These might include too much caffeine, hard-to-digest foods and inadequate sleep. Over time, stress builds. You may not realize the body is stressed; you might consider your experience typical rather than exceptional.

When I was experiencing food poisoning while pregnant, I had no idea my endocrine system was on the verge of collapse from stresses in my life. Unbeknownst to me, stress was simmering just under my awareness like a cauldron ready to bubble over. Lack of sleep from frequent work travel, stress from giving presentations to people twice my age, low-grade symptomless infections, life changes of marriage, selling a house and moving to a new community were all major stresses that rapidly accumulated.

If you're already depleted with low energy or you're hypersensitive, physical stresses can easily push you over the edge. One physical stress (especially lower-intensity chronic stressors) may not cause a problem, but as other stress builds and accumulates, so does the impact. Before you realize what's happening, the system starts to break down. Physical stresses may not be obvious but still impact the physical body and its energy.

Emotional stress risks becoming stored in the body when emotional experiences exceed your ability to cope. When this happens, energy becomes suppressed and not fully processed. In Western society, it's often considered healthy or desirable to suppress emotions without free expression. Control is valued, messy emotions are not. Many of us are taught that emotional outbursts are unwelcome, not allowed or tolerated. While social decorum is important to maintain order, we must find a way to process emotions that arise in order for the body to be healthy.

Fundamental principle: Expressed emotions leave; suppressed emotions are stored in the body.

Suppression creates a problem because the more you suppress, the larger the backlog. This can lead to emotion that builds and explodes when pressure mounts, often in a destructive and scary release. Explosive bursts of emotion can traumatize you and those around you. Expression may be met with ridicule, shame or even punishment. If parents aren't comfortable with emotional expression or frown upon it, children may hear statements such as, "You're too sensitive," or "If you don't stop crying, I'll give you something to really cry about." As adults, some of us may recall hearing these words in our own childhoods. We may reel for decades from these demands to keep a lid on our displays of emotion.

Children typically haven't mastered constructive emotional processing other than crying. All too often, crying is seen as weakness or disruption rather than the cleansing and releasing activity it really is. Emotional expression isn't just about emotional comfort; the unprocessed energy of difficult past experiences burdens more than our minds. Research proves the impact of adverse childhood events (ACES) on chronic health and disease later in life. Many studies have found an increased likelihood of cancer, heart disease and other leading causes of death correlated with childhood ACES[4,5,6].

In short, emotional stress stored in the body affects physical health later in life. It's imperative for your long-term health to find ways to constructively process emotion rather than store it. Remember the law of conservation of energy: emotional energy must be stored or expressed; it cannot simply disappear.

The Impact of Mental Health

Society commonly accepts mental stress as a health threat. Awareness of worker burnout and childhood anxiety is increasing. This is amazing progress. Not only does mental stress cause mental illness, it's also stored in the body and disrupts the body's physical ability to function.

Worry and anxiety are common problems. In fact, most children I work with carry significant amounts of these emotions. Sweaty palms, difficulty sleeping and indigestion are a few common symptoms that relate to energy blockages caused by mental stress. Research proves the impact mental stress has on health, including increased risk of cancer and cardiovascular disease. Any stress that causes the mind to ruminate or loop can affect the energy system and result in blockages that impact health. The effects of chronic stress on health are well documented in research, especially the work of Mariotti[7] and DeLongis[8].

Spiritual stress is harder to visualize but can still drain and block the body's energy. Difficult breakups, controlling parents, abusive relationships and attachments to past relationships create energetic connections that drain energy. Anyone who tries to control your behavior through force, manipulation or coercion is likely to be a drain on your energy unless you feel completely one hundred percent free with no emotional effect from these experiences.

Trauma can create connections to people you just can't get out of your head. There's an energetic reason for that—their energy is entangled with yours. Those connections disrupt your body's energy system, draining your energy until the connection is removed. In my healing sessions with clients, I often see attachments as cords that allow energy to leak from the body. Once the trauma is released, the cord is unhooked or falls away and you begin to retain your energy.

Sensitivity to Stress

It's important to understand the cumulative negative effect of stress. One stress alone may not impact your energy, but as stress hits repeatedly, it wears away your boundaries, draining reserves. When recovering from stress, your body is vulnerable and more sensitive to energy blockages from all sources.

> **Fundamental principle:** If your system is already weakened by stress, resilience is low. New stress has an amplified effect on your body and mind, making it easier to create new energy blockages.

Let's see how our ability to process stress works in everyday life. Suppose you're a creative four-year-old and decide to paint the kitchen cabinets with your new paint set. Your parent appears, gets angry and starts yelling at you. "I told you to paint only on paper," they scold. You feel ashamed and you were so excited about your creation!

At some point, your little self can't process all the big emotions bubbling up inside (shame, sadness) and your parent's strong emotion aimed at you (anger). Once you reach the point where you can't handle it anymore and are unable to process those feelings, you move into storage mode. You store your shame and your parent's anger in your body because it's not safe to express how you feel while your parent is so upset.

If this negative energy can't make its way out, it must be stored, according to the laws of physics. The point at which this happens depends on many factors, including your resilience, stress levels, emotional processing skills and the magnitude of your parent's reaction. Your stored emotion likely becomes one hundred percent subconscious and you don't know it's hiding inside you.

If you don't feel safe to express emotion or you're unable to do so, a shutdown of sorts occurs and the emotion is stored in your body. You likely learned from the actions of your caregivers that it isn't safe to express intense feelings and share how you really feel.

The ability to store intense emotion occurs for an important reason: it prevents damage to your personality. You burden your body with these experiences but storing them away has benefits. Your system hopes that eventually you'll have the skills and emotional support to safely process and release stored emotions. For now, though, this intense emotion is stored in your body.

> **Fundamental principle:** When emotion around a life experience exceeds your ability to process it, the energy must go somewhere, so it is stored in the body to protect you from overload and possibly lasting damage.

Over time, stored energy accumulates. Think of a cluttered garage or a basement in a house; the stored boxes make it difficult to move freely. As more clutter builds, it becomes impossible to move at all, blocking the natural flow of traffic. Soon, workarounds may be necessary, requiring more energy to carry out the same tasks.

The same is true for stored emotional baggage, which restricts energy flow in the body. The circulatory system is an example. Let's say you have a tourniquet on your arm. Constriction leads to reduced flow, which leads to less oxygen. Eventually, your hand will turn blue and suffer from inadequate circulation. The same is true with an energy blockage. Constriction from such a blockage will result in reduced circulation and eventually impact physical function if not resolved. Energy blockages set the stage for disease and health symptoms in the body.

Chapter 3: The Mind-Body Connection

Case Study: Chronic Pain

Sally came to me in desperation. She had tried everything for many years. She was working with a physical therapist, a chiropractor and a variety of doctors. She had dental problems in addition to the main reason for her visit with me—chronic pain. Her pain typically affected her belly and pelvis, where it moved around.

She sought relief with acupuncture, massage therapy, chiropractic care and other integrative therapies. A slew of Western medicine tests revealed no obvious cause for her pain. She herself had mind-body training and used any knowledge she could to help herself.

As we talked, she shared feelings about her difficult childhood. The only girl in a large family of boys, she was treated like Cinderella, made to cook and clean for the household. She was also keenly aware that her mom didn't want a girl. Because of others' actions and words, she felt deeply rejected by her mother. As an adult, while living in the Middle East with her child and husband, she became trapped during wartime. They suddenly found themselves in a combat zone and were forced to flee, leaving behind their personal possessions.

I found that Sally's emotional trauma was intertwined with the herpes zoster virus (shingles). She confirmed a significant case of shingles about the time her chronic pain started. As we worked to remove energy blocks to unburden the emotional trauma from her body and mind, repair her immune system and recognize how the virus affected her nervous system, her pain began to recede. After just one session, her family noted a much lighter appearance. She had worked tirelessly to find relief and finally felt a decrease in her pain and a new lightness in her spirit.

⮞

This case highlights the importance of addressing both the mind and body simultaneously. If Sally received only mental health therapy to work on her mental state, that might've helped her feel better, but it wouldn't have unraveled the impact on her immune system function, a key factor in fighting the viral infection causing her pain. On the other hand, working with just the chronic virus—perhaps with antiviral medications or herbs—wouldn't have addressed the impact of the trauma on her immune system and may have allowed a possible recurrence of the virus and her symptoms. The ability to address both the mind and body at the same time quickly got to the root cause of her symptoms and brought much-needed relief.

In high school, I dutifully sat in health class where I learned about body function and a little about mental illness. Nowhere was I taught about a connection. But the tides are changing: educators are starting to acknowledge the mind and body are indeed connected, as experts like Bessel van der Kolk and Louise Hay have made clear in their books[9,10]. Understanding this connection opens a whole world to navigating life with more health and balance.

The Hormonal Response to Stress

Imagine you're driving down the road when someone moves into your lane on a trajectory to hit your vehicle at 65 miles an hour. You frantically sound the horn and do your best to avoid an accident without causing one yourself. You narrowly avoid hitting the car and the guardrail.

In that moment, a cascade of hormonal shifts take place in your body. Your brain senses danger and releases a fight-or-flight alarm with chemical neurotransmitters and neuropeptides screaming *danger!* They flow through your body, changing brain chemistry. The magnitude of your reaction depends on your sensitivity and past exposure to stress.

Hormones tell the adrenal glands to release adrenaline and cortisol, starting a chain reaction in the cardiovascular, immune and nervous systems. Blood is shunted away from digestion and directed to the heart and muscles to prime them for action. The heart beats faster, blood pressure rises and you are ready to spring into action. In this state, normal digestion can't happen, blood pressure and heart rate increase and the body can't relax. The mind just created a cascade of physical responses.

Other examples of the mind-body connection include anxiety causing stomachache, mental stress causing tension headache and a stressful day disrupting your ability to sleep. In these situations, an agitated mind creates an effect on the body.

Consider a night where you toss and turn and wake at 3:00 a.m., unable to sleep for the remainder of the night. You're exhausted when it's time to get up, so you start the day tired and frazzled. By the time you arrive at work, you have a headache, stomachache and your physical energy is low. You likely have trouble focusing and you feel overwhelmed. If someone tries to have a stressful conversation with you, you may feel reactive and emotional. In this case, the physical lack of sleep affects your mood and reactions. Your body created a cascade of mental responses in reaction to physical stress.

> **Fundamental principle:** The body influences the mind and the mind influences the body. Medical research proves that the mind-body connection affects the body's physical function.

Subconscious Defined

Your mind consists of two aspects: the conscious and the subconscious. The conscious mind is more easily accessible to us because we are aware of its activities. But what about the part we are not aware of? The Oxford Language program defines the subconscious as "of or concerning the part of the mind of which one is not fully aware, but which influences one's actions and feelings." Since 80% or more of your brain's daily function is subconscious, this part of you is significant. In fact, it drives the show.

According to Dr. Fred Luskin of Stanford University, the average person has between 40,000 and 60,000 thoughts per day, ninety percent of which are subconscious. That means you're under tremendous influence from your subconscious mind, but most of the time you're not aware of what exists there.

I like to think of this part of you as an attic or basement. You may remember what's in some of the boxes, but not all. However, they reside within you, influencing the way you perceive the outside world, how you feel about yourself and what you feel is possible in your life. It's not easy to access what is stored here; after all, it's subconscious! In my experience, the mind can store stressful experiences where they remain hidden from awareness, making it harder to access without professional help.

The subconscious mind carries a lot of hidden influence. That nagging voice in the back of your mind, the whisper of self-doubt and the uneasy feeling in the belly likely have roots in your subconscious mind. Your subconscious mind wields a lot of power and influence.

In early childhood, you learn by watching and listening to those around you. Is the world safe and welcoming? Are you worthy of success? Is your body strong? The thoughts you have now about these questions are rooted in the way your primary caregivers felt about the world around you and what they silently demonstrated through perceptions, words and actions. Before you had a logical mind to decide if a particular worldview made sense, you absorbed it through this conditioning and it became a part of you.

Conditioning creates thoughts spoken by your mind. These thoughts generate emotional energy. So, if your primary caregiver was fearful and felt the world was dangerous, belief patterns and thought systems were programmed in your mind, creating perceptions of the world as unsafe. That perception creates emotions of anxiety and fear, which sets the stage for energy disruptions.

The Power of the Senses

Senses are filtered by the subconscious mind's view of the world. Consider the following simple example.

My father's cat suddenly began vomiting frequently. A family member worried that the cat might have a severe health condition. This family member was a doctor who treats severe illnesses every day. She is conditioned to fear the worst about health. I don't spend all day working with severely ill people in hospital settings, so I have a different perception. I felt the cat was likely overeating. Our different perspectives and experiences affected the way we perceived the simple event of the cat vomiting frequently.

If your mind and resulting thoughts feel afraid, your senses are more likely to perceive risk, danger and vulnerability to reinforce feeling unsafe. On the other hand, if your mind feels safe, your senses will likely perceive safety and protection. This explains how two people can see the same exact event with vastly different experiences of it. If you have siblings, you may have completely different memories of the same past event. Sensory perceptions and stored past experiences act as filters to allow two people to observe the exact same event but form vastly different memories of it.

If you don't understand how influential your past experiences and sense filters are and how they influence perception, you may believe that what you sense is one hundred percent truth. Many years ago, I drove to school each afternoon to pick up my child. I waited dutifully in the pickup line until I got to the front of the school. A teacher was there, calling students and escorting them to their waiting rides. A certain teacher generally had a stern demeanor, but one week I honestly felt she was mad at me. Her mannerisms and the way she spoke seemed to project displeasure. I wondered what I might have done. For the next three days, each afternoon I saw this teacher, I felt the same way.

On Friday of that week, I had an energy healing session working on my perceptions and anxiety about people not liking me. That very afternoon, all my perceptions of this teacher's actions completely changed. She was warm and friendly to me and she appeared happy. Maybe she had four grumpy days. Perhaps. Did I just sense inaccurately through a filter of fear that people won't like me? Highly likely.

It's important to realize that perceptions are subjective. The power of the mind and stored beliefs about the world can strongly influence perceived reality.

Anatomy of the Mind-Body Connection

We've talked about the mind creating physical responses in the body that lead to energy blockages. Let's go a little deeper. When you feel an emotion from any source, the brain and nervous system react.

As discussed earlier, research proves that emotion impacts the physical function of the body[11]. The cardiovascular, endocrine and autonomic nervous systems all respond with physical changes to stress. It's generally accepted that an emotional experience results in three responses: your subjective experience (how it feels), a physiological response (what it affects in your body) and a behavioral or expressive response (action you take as a result of the emotional experience)[12].

Think of it this way: every emotional experience you have includes what you feel, what it causes inside you, and how you react to it. These experiences influence your brain and nervous system. Your brain chemistry, neurotransmitters and endocrine system change. Your entire body is affected, all from an emotional experience. The same is also true if the emotional energy becomes stored in the subconscious mind or body. There's a significant proven link between how you feel and how your brain and body react.

The Role of Negative Emotions

Emotions are a normal part of being human. If you didn't have them, you'd likely have significant disorders of either mind or body. People are often led to believe that negative emotions are just a nuisance, but they have a definite purpose: they share valuable information with you. In fact, emotions are a primary means of communication from body to mind. Yes, you read that correctly: negative emotions serve a valuable purpose by telling you non-verbally that something needs your attention. (After all, the body can't just start a dialogue with you).

Difficult emotions can highlight when change is needed. A parent feels frustrated because their young child argues and doesn't listen. No matter how many times the parent wants cooperation, the child can't control themself. The parent's internal feelings of frustration are an indication of needed change, in this case, pinpointing a need to make a change in the external environment. Perhaps the child needs a nap, food, or perhaps the parent needs to set better boundaries. Either way, frustration indicates that change needs to happen.

Difficult emotion can also indicate stored energy buried beneath the surface, just like the tip of an iceberg. I call this triggering—when a seemingly small life experience triggers a much larger-than-expected emotional response. While it is unpleasant, triggering is a huge gift from your subconscious mind informing you of unconscious energy affecting you.

Triggering provides an opportunity to relive a suppressed emotion from the past. It's certainly not fun to experience difficult emotion, but the result is an opportunity to heal in body and mind for good. Remember, an emotion becomes suppressed when you're unable to fully process it in the moment. Your subconscious mind stores the energy to prevent damage to your psyche. Suppression is a form of protection. Triggering is the opposite action: it helps reconnect you to the stored energy so it can be healed completely.

How can you spot a trigger? When you have an oversized emotional reaction to something in your life that doesn't seem like a big deal, you are probably triggered. Let's say you read a disturbing news article and for some reason, you just can't forget about it. It keeps popping up in your mind, causing you to feel agitated, anxious or fearful. You try to put it behind you, but it keeps coming to mind with an emotional charge. The article struck a chord within you and you can't seem to stop its reverberation.

This is a sign that something hiding beneath the surface has been activated in your subconscious mind. The suppressed emotion was in your body and mind the entire time, hiding. Triggering shines a light on suppressed emotion within your body that is ready to be healed.

> **Fundamental principle:** An oversized emotional reaction to an everyday event is a sign of triggering when stored emotion lies beneath the surface, ready to be cleared.

Case Study: Triggering

As I walked into the room with Jennifer, she was visibly upset. "Something happened and I'm afraid to tell you." I reassured her that it was safe for her to share it with me so I could help her. "But it's so upsetting. I don't want you to be upset by it."

I again reassured her that whatever it was, I could handle hearing it to help her feel better. After all, she was here with me, the day after this event, so I felt reassured that I could help her resolve her feelings. She went on to describe a terrifying situation of a close friend who was involved in a domestic dispute.

The friend's husband tried to significantly harm her, but she managed to escape. While this event was difficult and unpleasant, it didn't trigger an emotional reaction in me the way it had for Jennifer. She felt one hundred percent triggered, unsafe and anxious. Her friend's experience struck an emotional chord within her own subconscious mind; otherwise, the story would not have bothered her so profoundly.

In Jennifer's session, we focused on her fear of feeling unsafe with family members from events in her past, as well as the current concern she felt for the safety of her friend. We neutralized the trauma of the situation, both past and present. At the end of her session with me, she felt calm and able to support her friend.

∽

The Role of Negative Thoughts

The mind holds vast control over your daily experiences. According to the National Science Foundation, the average person has thousands of thoughts per day, with 80% negative and 95% the same as the day before. To make matters worse, approximately 90% are subconscious, so you're likely not aware of the negativity your mind is focusing on.

Take a moment to absorb what this means: stories flow through your mind throughout the day that rule how you view the world. Most of the time, you're not aware of the story. The flow of negative thought in many of us is like a river, continuous and steadfast.

Negative thoughts can pop up many times throughout the day, in moments as simple as what to pack for lunch or as complex as whether to buy a home. If you're someone whose mind has a hard time quieting, your exposure to negative thoughts is likely amplified. Your body and mind carry a burden of negativity created by beliefs from past conditioning, often that you don't consciously believe, that is continuously flowing from your subconscious mind. The anxiety produced by these thoughts, even if they fly under the radar, accumulates and impacts your physical body. Negative thoughts such as "I'm not safe" or "There won't be enough" or "Life is always harder for me" add up and lead to stomach ulcers, irritable bowel disease, anxiety disorders, adrenal burnout and more.

> **Fundamental principle:** Thoughts create emotional energy that affect your body.

As if the continuous flow of negative thought weren't enough, consider that thought creates emotion and influences perception. The thought *What if I'm wrong?* creates anxiety and self-doubt. Think of a time you were unsure of a decision. How did that feel? If you felt anxiety, worry or stress, the words *What if I'm wrong?* might have been playing in your head sparking those feelings. You may have been aware of the story or maybe not. Either way, emotion affects your body. But that's not all. This *What if I'm wrong?* thought pattern also influences your perceptions of the world around you. The thought *What if I'm wrong?* at the conscious or subconscious level causes you to feel a lack of confidence or doubt about your judgment or even the belief that making a decision is unsafe.

This thought pattern holds you back from your true potential, all because a subconscious thought is influencing your perceptions of reality. This pattern, of course, is not good. You wouldn't consciously choose to have your life ruled by old childhood beliefs or by your family's past. It's time to discover and heal negative beliefs to allow yourself to live on your own terms.

Let's take a moment to discuss where negative thoughts come from. As mentioned earlier, research shows that familial beliefs influence our worldview. Add the fact that your logical mind doesn't develop until well later. You don't have the ability to decide if the incoming worldview resonates with you before the logical mind is developed. The worldview you're presented with gets adopted as your own.

The viewpoints and behaviors of your major childhood caregivers have a significant impact. Do these caregivers feel safe when they go shopping? Are they worried about your well-being? Do they let you play freely or hover, worrying about you getting hurt? Is the body regarded as safe and strong or do they worry that something might be wrong?

The child learns by osmosis just by being in the family environment, listening and watching the adults around them. Belief systems and thought patterns are learned by watching, much like walking or speaking. If a pattern of feeling unsafe is mirrored by caregivers, the child may form similar subconscious belief systems.

Another important source of thought patterns is family history. Perhaps your grandmother experienced food shortages during the Great Depression. The emotional energy of these events can carry forward, creating thought patterns. The fear of not having enough food creates patterns of thought and action that can then be passed down.

For example, your mother may prepare three times the amount of food needed for a family gathering. Perhaps you fear not being able to find ingredients, so you buy more than needed. The energy of food shortage has traveled through three generations, creating various patterns of food hoarding. It's important to note that world views often originate from an experience you've never felt personally. Someone in your family did, though, and that energy travels forward. To free the body, energy anchoring the thought pattern must be neutralized.

To summarize, the mind retains negative thoughts. Negative thoughts create emotions that affect the body. Once the body is burdened, weakened, depleted, stressed or otherwise off balance, it loses its ability to cope. Stress adds up, and energy blockages result. Over time, an energy blockage affects your mental and physical health.

The good news is that you do not need to carry the past forward. In the chapters that follow, I'll explain how to access the subconscious mind and remove negative belief patterns, removing energy blockages and freeing your body.

Chapter 4: Cringe-Worthy Memories Matter

Your past impacts your health. In earlier chapters, we discussed unresolved emotion and how it is stored in the body. Stored energy is known to contribute to chronic illness, setting the stage for all sorts of health challenges, including addiction, cancer, cardiovascular disease, and mental health illnesses. What we often don't realize is that change is possible! Potent tools exist to release the power of the past without having to re-experience trauma.

> **Fundamental principle:** Energy healing can release the power of your past, without you having to relive it.

Do you have a past memory that makes you cringe when you think about it? Find a memory like this from any time in your life. The surge of emotion you feel when thinking about this past memory—perhaps embarrassment, anger, shame, or guilt—is stored emotional energy. It's the same force that causes the momentary cringe. It's stored somewhere in your body, disrupting communication and function.

With an energy healing tool, the electrical charge caused by this memory can be released. Once the energy is neutralized, the memory will still exist, but it won't have emotion attached to it. Instead, it will feel completely neutral when you bring the memory to mind. Once this happens, the body's function returns to normal, no longer burdened by the disruptive emotional energy. That's how energy medicine works. We've talked about how one memory can disrupt energy. Let's apply this principle more broadly.

Your past matters. The past experience with a volatile parent whose mood flipped from neutral to tyrant on a dime impacts your mind and nervous system. If you felt you had to walk on eggshells for fear of their explosive emotion, this likely caused stress that impacted your nervous system, digestive system and sense of safety. The lingering subconscious programming of feeling unsafe can continue to cause nervous system stress years later. Fear is not the only emotion that leaves an imprint. Consider grief. Leaving your best childhood friend due to a family move impacts the heart and your ability to connect to others.

Your sense of power and safety comes from your formative years. If you were bullied in school, your digestive, reproductive and endocrine systems may be affected. Criticism you may have endured from family members, teachers or close friends impacts your confidence, thyroid, adrenal and digestive health. These are just a few examples showing how your past affects your body's function. Experiences create a cocktail of stored emotion, which can affect belief systems and cause energy disruptors to live in your body, influencing how you perceive and relate to the world around you.

How you felt in the past matters. I often tell my clients that what happened is not as important as how you felt and what you perceived. Did you feel your mom showed favoritism to your siblings and treated you unfairly? Did your siblings deny it was true and think you were crazy? It doesn't matter! All that matters is how you felt and what you perceived. This is what must be addressed energetically if you wish to embrace full wellness.

Add this important fact: it doesn't even matter what you feel now. If you and your siblings get along great and this is all in the past, that's wonderful. However, if you felt that way in your childhood and you have not found a way to release this emotional energy, it must be accessed and released for you to find complete freedom.

Your conscious mind's current state doesn't negate the past energy stored in your body. There is a common misconception that if the conscious mind is okay, the body is okay. If the emotional energy is stored, the body is affected until it is released.

> **Fundamental principle:** Your conscious mind's current state doesn't negate energy stored in your body from the past.

Your experience matters. The intention of others doesn't matter, nor the actual events. How you experience and perceive the world around you is what affects your energy.

Case Study: Perception Matters

After picking up my preschooler on the way home from work, I entered the house and immediately fell onto the couch. I was pregnant and nauseated with all-day morning sickness and extremely low energy levels.

"I want to play, Mommy," my four-year-old begged. Miserable, I responded, "I don't feel well and need to rest. Play here beside me."

His behavior changed after a couple of weeks of this situation. "I'm sorry, Mommy, for making you feel sick."

Whoa. Did I miss something? How did my child decide he was responsible for my nausea and fatigue? This experience taught me a valuable lesson: perceptions and beliefs, even if far from the truth, are still your reality and valid from a healing standpoint. Your experience of events matters, reality not so much.

✦

A special word about trauma is warranted. People endure significant hardships in life. If a particular experience exceeds your ability to process the event, it can be locked away for storage in your body. The more intense the experience, the larger the risk of energy blockage.

Any experience can create disruptions, even events you may not consider as trauma, especially if chronic in nature. Birth trauma, abuse, victimization, bullying and divorce are obvious major stresses that can affect you deeply. Major illness also falls into this category, often leaving trauma in the mind and body. Exclusion, criticism, adoption or abandonment can also have a deep energetic impact. The factor that most controls the energetic impact of an experience is whether you were able to fully process the events at the time.

In my practice, a new client will often tell me they were abused, then quickly state they understood what their parents endured and they've forgiven them. Forgiveness and understanding are noble and likely achieved through a lot of healing and hard work, but I ask these clients to consider: did you release the stored energy of emotional abuse from all parts of your body and mind, including the subconscious?

In general, most people understand their parents did their best, given their own trauma and circumstances. However, that ability to logically understand their struggles doesn't negate your experience. You may have deeper understanding born from the wisdom of time, but what about the inner child who suffered harm? That part of you and the stored energy from the experiences must be healed to free your health and bring lasting peace.

We've talked about unprocessed emotion stored in the body. Traumatic experiences can also become tagged to the senses. Specific images, sounds and activities can all trigger unresolved trauma in the body. That energy must be released everywhere it's stored in order for you to achieve complete closure and freedom. Yes, complete freedom is possible.

If you're unable to release a traumatic experience completely, it may be because your body is holding onto hidden energy, even though your mind is ready to be free. Energy healing is a highly effective way to neutralize the effects of stored emotions without having to relive the painful past. In fact, with energy healing, traumatic memories do not need to be discussed at all to heal the blocked energy.

Case Study: Trauma and the Sense of Touch

Tina arrived at my office. She was visibly anxious as she sat down in my treatment room and told me, "I have the most supportive, gentle husband but I'm feeling uncomfortable being touched and I think I know why." She went on to explain she knew she was the victim of abuse in her past but had no recollection of the actual events.

Her intimate relationship with her husband was suffering. She felt unsafe and anxious when touched, even though her husband was completely loving and respectful. She felt the abuse was affecting her and wanted to leave it behind for good. I assured her I could gently remove the trauma without any discussion. And that is just what we did.

We neutralized energy around the past abuse, especially feeling unsafe and unprotected by the adults in her life. We also cleared the trauma tagged onto her sense of touch. Each time she was touched, she had subconsciously relived the trauma of being powerless and unsafe. We cleared all that energy without having to focus on past details or actual events. With just a few sessions, she found the freedom she sought. She became able to be touched in her loving relationship without mental or physical discomfort.

❧

Family dynamics matter. We've discussed how your unique experience matters. Difficult family dynamics deeply influence how you feel consciously and subconsciously. If you have a loving family but someone is always on the verge of an explosion due to overwhelm, you may feel fear and anxiety. Your body doesn't know when it will be unsafe, so it looks for danger signs and inadvertently becomes locked in hypervigilance mode, constantly walking on eggshells.

The severity and frequency of emotional explosions matter and influence the magnitude of impact on your energy. The more frequent and intense the explosions, the more likely you suffer from some sort of post-traumatic stress disorder (PTSD). The less frequent and less intense the episodes, the more likely you are to have anxiety triggered by certain situations (i.e., conflict). Fighting between parents, even if only verbal, can leave childhood imprints of feeling unsafe.

If your past had events you weren't able to fully process at the time, your body may still carry the disruptive energies of anxiety or hypervigilance. Energy is typically amplified for children because they're trapped in the situation. Adults and older teens may have an escape mechanism, and the effect on their system may be less.

Another important family dynamic is control. Being controlled—whether through punishment, shaming or judgment—creates energetic patterns and blocks. If you faced criticism, high expectations or disapproval—especially if you struggled to meet those standards—feelings of unworthiness or shame may have affected you. These emotional energies are important to consider.

Children's early attachment to their primary caregivers focuses on one thing: being cared for. As an infant, attachment means life or death. In young childhood, it is still the child's survival mechanism to receive love and approval.

If judgment was present in your family culture—if you were not allowed to be your authentic self or had to conform to family expectations—you likely carry blockages related to that energy.

Suppression of your authentic self, lack of confidence in your own judgment and strong fear of making mistakes are just some of the deeply-held patterns that can result from family judgment. A blend of belief systems and unprocessed emotions can affect major systems in your body, including the thyroid, adrenal, reproductive, digestive, respiratory and nervous systems. This isn't just a story in your mind about your past; it's also a story in your body that must be released.

In situations of challenging family dynamics, the body can get "addicted" to stress chemicals. This means that once you've left the stressful environment, your body may feel the need to manifest circumstances that generate similar stress. This is entirely subconscious; I don't know anyone who would knowingly choose to create stress. Alternately, another common barrier is a "joy threshold," a barrier that functions like a tripwire. When life gets too good, you bring yourself crashing back down by creating circumstances that sabotage feeling happy.

Have you ever been on a vacation and had a lovely day, only to have someone get injured, or an argument ensues that suddenly dampens the joy? When your joy is dramatically dampened by the injury or the argument and you're unable to get past the temporary frustration, you've hit your joy threshold. When joy thresholds hit, they bring you back to your usual comfort zone. Let's clarify one thing: no one would consciously limit their happiness or choose to let something ruin their joy. This is a subconscious pattern born of past stress. You're powerless against it until the energy is cleared.

Joy Threshold

My husband and I met mountain biking. He was an avid biker for years and I had just started to enjoy the sport when I met him. In our first few years together, we spent most of our free time mountain biking with friends on amazing trails in Virginia. It was so fulfilling on many levels: fun social outings, great exercise, beautiful nature views. Fast forward fifteen years, three kids and a long health journey later—we no longer did much biking.

One spring morning, the weather cooperated. It wasn't too wet or cold. The sun was shining, the air fresh. It was a perfect day after the cold winter. The whole family decided to ride together on a local trail. Everyone was excited.

My husband, our resident bike mechanic, started preparing the bikes for the ride. First, one bike had a flat tire and he changed it. As I herded the children and loaded the car, he realized another bike had a flat tire. He changed it. Mind you, we hadn't even left the house yet! Almost a full hour later, he had changed three flat tires. Finally, with a huge sigh of relief, we piled in the car and got underway.

The ride started off pleasantly enough. My kids' ages span almost twelve years, so the teenager wanted to go faster while the preschooler wanted to dawdle. My teen and his dad went ahead. About half an hour later, we saw them coming toward us walking their bikes. Guess what happened? They both got flat tires on the trail! On that occasion, flat tires generated stress and kept the joy level down. When your energy is comfortable at a certain frequency, situations can arise that prevent joy. Accidents, injuries or unanticipated schedule disruptions are just some of the situations where events suddenly don't go according to plan, resulting in a day that doesn't meet your expectations.

✦

Luckily, a tool such as energy healing can release past energies from the body and reset thresholds, so creating stress is no longer necessary. The body stops subconsciously looking for ways to repeat familiar patterns. Energy healing can help you find complete freedom from past stress. The body can then reset cell receptors that are addicted to stress hormones. This allows full release, not only from your mental and emotional self, but also the physical body.

Next, I will introduce healing tools to identify what might be burdening your energy. Remember, awareness is often 80% of the solution. It's time to learn some of the fundamentals of this process.

Chapter 5: What Is Energy Healing?

We've talked about your body's energy field and some of the factors that create energy blockages. Luckily, there's a way to remove these blockages to repair the body. In short, you can undo damage caused by your life experiences. At the most basic level, energy healing is a method of working with the body's energy field to bring about healing. It removes energy blockages and disruptions so the body and mind can restore balance.

The practitioner uses focused intention to create healing. Quantum physics proves that energy follows intention. If you focus your intention, you can direct your energy there to create change. Energy healers develop and hone this skill to use focused energy to bring healing to the entire system, body, mind and spirit.

Along with considering the whole person, healing energetic disruption addresses the root cause of illness rather than simply treating symptoms. The body is strengthened from the ground up. By working on the root cause of disruption, various seemingly unrelated parts of the body benefit.

For example, I worked with a child to improve his verbal tics. During his first session, I felt a need to balance a disruption for his mother. I cleared her trauma from her parents' difficult divorce when she was 13. When the mother and child returned for the follow-up session, she shared that her asthma vanished after our work. During the session, I never worked on asthma or her breathing; I didn't even know she had the condition! Her body organically strengthened with the removal of the energy from her past, allowing healing of a seemingly unrelated symptom.

Another benefit of energy healing is that healing persists because we aren't just treating symptoms. As energy blockages clear, the body returns to normal flow and function. The results can be astounding and long-lasting because we're rebooting the body's innate ability to heal.

> **Fundamental principle:** Energy follows intention.

As stored energy clears, the body lightens. Picture an attic filled with clutter until an organizing crew spends several hours clearing it. Imagine the "after" picture of the attic being tidy and neat. Energy work does the work of that crew for your emotional and energetic baggage. The body begins to function more normally, the mind becomes clearer and symptoms begin to resolve. Let's consider an example.

Jim had stomach ulcers. Since his teenage years, he felt anxious about his schoolwork. He studied more than his friends because he was afraid he'd get low grades that would hurt his chances of going to college. As a result of his worries, his stomach produced too much acid, leading to stomach ulcers and digestive pain. If Jim sought medical help, his symptoms would likely be treated with an acid-lowering or acid-blocking drug. This would decrease his stomach acid and improve his symptoms. But the root cause of the issue would still be there: his overactive mind and anxiety.

If Jim stopped his medication, the symptoms would likely return. Energy healing works with the root cause of anxiety and worry. In Jim's case, it slowed negative thinking and therefore naturally decreased his abnormal stomach acid production. Subconscious beliefs, past experiences and perhaps family patterns were likely the root of his bodily dysfunction. As stored energies were released, the root cause of his health symptoms could heal, leaving him free of ulcers without medication.

Self-Help Resources

Energy healing consists of a vast array of healing tools. Some are simple and easily implemented. Others require in-depth training and skill development.

Later in this book you'll learn a process to work with energy in your body and experience a complete energy medicine session firsthand. I refer to energy medicine as precisely focused energy healing with the goal of achieving clinically significant physical healing.

Self-help resources are a powerful way to take charge of your health. In the coming chapters, you will learn focused self-help resources that can be used to soothe the body and mind in order to heal energy but first let's start with simple processes.

One of the easiest ways to calm your body is to calm your mind. Meditation, intentional breathing, yoga, qi gong and prayer have the power to immediately change your body's energy. In addition to their intended purpose, these tools quiet the mind to stop the flow of negative emotional energy generated by negative thought.

Turning off the spigot of negative energy is powerful and should not be underestimated. Your nervous system immediately moves into rest-and-digest mode. This causes a cascade of positive effects, such as calming the immune and cardiovascular systems, downregulating the nervous system and boosting digestion. Your energy immediately responds with calmer feelings.

These activities are accessible, free, easy to learn and don't require sophisticated knowledge or skills. You can watch a YouTube video, listen to a free meditation app or search for breathing exercises all without leaving the comfort of your home. Also, consider any other activity that quiets your mind, like hiking, gardening, creating art, walking in nature or mindful exercise.

These tools are great adjuncts to other treatments and general balancers that help you feel better when you need a boost. If your mind is quiet and focused on the present moment, you're soothing your energy.

Energy Source Used in Healing

Clients frequently ask if I tire while conducting healing sessions. The answer is a big, resounding no! In fact, when I had morning sickness and low energy while pregnant, I would wake thinking *I'm not sure I have the energy to get through the day* only to feel much more energized with less nausea after working with clients.

Healing others gives me energy! I do not give away my personal energy to heal others. I use focused intention to bring healing by repairing blockages with universal energy from the quantum field. I use this energy to power up and boost significantly depleted patients. Universal energy is like an energy pipeline accessible at any time.

Research proves the existence of the quantum energy field that underlies physical experience. The *Cliff Notes* version is that energy surrounds you at all times. You use it to create every experience you have. Healers use this energy to deliver healing. An excellent book to learn more about research proving the existence of quantum energy is *The Field* by Lynn McTaggart.

When I work with clients, I often use light or representations of energy during energy healing sessions. I may see energy as a tangle of yarn, so I pull out the disorganized energy. Sometimes I see a vat of viscous liquid needing to be drained from the body or a cord attached to a former controlling partner that needs to be disconnected. In my work, however the energy initially presents itself, blockages move out, energy drains fall away and balanced energy starts flowing properly to restore health.

Clients often ask if my work in any way conflicts with their religious beliefs. This is an understandable concern. I can assure you there is no conflict with any religion that I'm aware of. I've delivered energy healing sessions to devout members of many religions: Islam, Christianity, Judaism, Catholicism, Hinduism and probably others. Never have I witnessed a client who didn't benefit from healing bodily energy blockages.

Religion is a language of spirituality. Energy healing is a tool to heal the body and spirit. In my opinion, they are synonymous with the goal of a happy, healthy person capable of making the world a better place. I think of religion as a language to connect to source energy.

Source energy has a number of different names: God, Allah, Gaia, Mother Earth, divine, source, all that is, life force and quantum field. It doesn't matter what you call it. What matters is this: source energy supplies all you need to heal your body and mind. As you release lower vibration energy blockages, your vibration rises, aligning you with health, joy and peace. In short, you feel good and you can help others feel good. This enables you to change the world by adding a positive contribution and living your soul's purpose.

Chapter 6: Be an Energy Intuitive

We discussed the body's innate ability to heal and how its intelligence pinpoints energy blockages. We also discussed how symptoms share vital information with you. Luckily, the body can share information in efficient ways that don't require pain or hardship. Meet your intuitive senses. We all have intuitive sense; you have likely used it in everyday life, though you probably didn't realize it. Let's dig into the details.

You Can Hear Intuition

Before you decide you have no intuition, bear with me. Intuition is a quiet, subtle broadcaster of always-flowing information.

Imagine listening to a radio in your kitchen while you move from one place to another, gathering ingredients and utensils while you chop, cook and retrieve dishes. All those activities generate a lot of noise! Cabinet doors close, water glasses clink and water from the spigot splashes loudly when it hits the sink. You stop for just a moment to determine your next step and playing quietly in the background is a song you love. You didn't hear it until you paused.

The same is true with intuition. It's low-volume and hard to hear in the busyness of day-to-day life. Noise and thoughts block intuition; it's there, waiting for you to tap into the signal. But you have to calm the static and noise to hear it.

It's not just life's busyness that blocks intuition; it's also stress of all kinds: mental, emotional, physical and spiritual. If you're in physical distress, you will likely have difficulty receiving intuition. If you eat foods that don't serve you, have chronic infections, get poor sleep or feel overwhelmed, those factors generate noise that can block intuition from being heard.

Intuition is related to energy. When stress is removed, energy calms, the body calms and your intuition becomes audible. It's a wonderful side effect of healing.

The way to start sensing intuition is simple: calm your mind and body. You're most likely to hear intuition when you're present in the moment. Find an activity where your mind can be quiet and awake. Examples are driving without music, meditating, sitting quietly without particular focus, walking, being in nature or exercising if you aren't distracted by TV, music or other noise. These moments allow the mind to be quiet, allowing intuition to break through to conscious awareness. Alternatively, calm the mind and focus on your breath for five to fifteen minutes. That's all you need to help your mind learn to slow down.

If you've struggled to tap into your intuition because you doubt yourself, you're not alone. The good news is this intuitive block is just energy, not a reflection of your abilities. With a few pointers, you can begin nurturing self-trust.

Self-Doubt: The Saboteur

Self-doubt regarding intuition focuses on three key areas: questioning your ability to engage with something unconventional, confusion about whether your perceptions are genuinely intuitive and the challenge of achieving emotional clarity to minimize bias. Let's briefly discuss these roadblocks.

Self-doubt is an insidious emotion pervading all sorts of daily activities; intuition is just one. If you frequently have a voice in your head criticizing, doubting, belittling or otherwise denying your ability to be strong and authentically yourself, this is an area needing healing focus.

Realize that self-doubt is just a story; it isn't true. In later chapters, we will address this head-on. In the meantime, recognize beliefs that easily block or unfairly discredit intuitive information: self-doubt, self-criticism, fear of making a mistake, being punished or other limiting beliefs. The awareness that your thoughts aren't always true can quickly diffuse the power of negative thinking and reclaim your power.

Action is often the best remedy for self-doubt. As we will discuss in a moment, intuition is a muscle that builds with use, getting stronger over time. Just as with learning to walk or learning a new language, at first our efforts feel clumsy and choppy. With practice, strength and skill builds.

Intuition can be quiet, unobtrusive and hard to hear, so it's easy to miss completely or doubt its validity, but it isn't a figment of your imagination. The mind may think all that exists is the five physical senses; however, ample research shows that intuition exists, structured and highly effective, including the work of McTaggart[13] and Zander[14].

You are late leaving for a day of sightseeing. As you ready to leave home, you hear a small voice in your head saying *bring water*. You dismiss this voice, figuring there will be water available at your destination. You don't bother to go back inside, relieved to finally be on your way.

Later you are thirsty. You look and realize you cannot find a store or water fountain at the museum. You suddenly remember the voice and realize listening to it would've made your life easier.

There's a simple way to know what is intuition and what isn't. It works most of the time. Let me share an important principle.

Fundamental principle: When you sense something, is your mind busy or quiet? If quiet, that something is likely intuition. If busy, it could be a creation of the mind.

If your mind is in a calm, focused state and you sense something, it's likely intuition. Your mind didn't create it, because your mind was clear and relaxed. If your mind is busy thinking and churning and you sense something, it could be generated by your mind. This is the most reliable way I know to determine the origin of the information you sense.

If you wake in that in-between time when you're not fully asleep or fully awake and you sense something, it's intuition. If you're sitting quietly and you sense something, it's intuition. If, on the other hand, you're sitting in the car worrying about your to-do list and you sense something, it may be a creation of the mind. If you're at work feeling anxious about a decision you need to make and you sense something, it's likely the mind at work.

Another important factor to consider is your emotional involvement. If you're trying to decide if a particular food is good or bad for you, that decision could be emotionally charged. If so, asking and hoping for guidance can be muddied by your desires. We're human after all and intuition is received through the human instrument.

If you believe something isn't right for you, that will affect the clarity of the intuition you receive. That's why it's key for the person receiving information to be as clear as possible, as free from bias and preconceived thought as possible. And know that even if an experienced practitioner is giving you intuitive input, their clarity will affect their results. Nothing is one hundred percent accurate, including science.

The Intuitive Senses

Your brain is built to receive intuitive information through senses, much like the five physical senses you're familiar with. Information comes into your awareness through the physical senses of touch, taste, smell, hearing and sight. Your body senses stimuli, passes that information to the brain to be processed and decides what action to take, if any. This is the path of the physical senses and perceptions.

A similar process exists for intuitive information. Consider the following intuitive senses: smell, taste, knowing, sight, hearing and feeling. These intuitive senses share information, the same way their physical counterparts do. When I first learned about intuition, I felt there was no way I could receive insight through these senses. I was too focused on my five senses and intellect; after all, I have two engineering degrees and was taught to understand the world around me through analysis and thought. Over time, with practice, I learned to listen in a different way. Before you have similar thoughts about your intuitive abilities, you are likely already receiving information from these senses; you just may not realize it.

Consider the sense of hearing. Sound waves travel through the ear, and your body converts the sound to nerve impulses (energy) that travel along the auditory nerve to the brain. Your brain receives the information and processes it. This is how sound waves in your environment become information in your brain. You hear with your ears and your brain receives information that it brings to your conscious awareness: beautiful music, children laughing, loud traffic. You may also hear sounds that never quite make it to your conscious awareness, such as someone talking to you while you're daydreaming or the contents of a video call while you're trying to respond to an important email.

Have you ever heard something but can't find evidence of it? Perhaps music, someone talking or even hearing music lyrics or words in your head? This is your intuition (and no, you're not crazy).

Intuition is a subtle supply of information. It works perfectly for healing and everyday life purposes. You may feel confirmation that a decision is positive, sense where you left your keys or suddenly realize you haven't called your mom today. These gentle bits of information guide you where you need to go, without triggering anxiety or feelings of being mentally unstable. This type of intuition creates feelings of clarity, support and knowing what is best for you.

Before we take a more detailed look at the intuitive senses, a word of advice: allow whatever comes to your awareness to be okay. If you find yourself thinking, judging or comparing, notice what the mind is doing and bring yourself back to the present moment.

Once you receive intuitive information, decide what to do with it. Acting, ignoring and doubting are all options available to you. The ultimate decision of how to handle this information is entirely up to you; just because you receive intuition doesn't mean you have to act on it. It's entirely your choice how you wish to proceed. Let's go through the primary intuitive senses and how they might share information with you for healing purposes.

Sense of Feeling: Clairsentience

The intuitive sense of feeling is my favorite intuitive sense, the one I use in every single healing session. According to Dictionary.com, clairsentience is the ability to feel or sense information through extrasensory means, allowing you to perceive information beyond your physical senses. If this sense is active for you, you may feel a sensation in your body: tightness, pressure, heat, cold, buzzing, churning. These sensations can be mild or intense, sometimes even bordering on pain. You may feel air blowing across your face, something being pulled or drained out of the body, your hands buzzing or even a hand resting on your shoulder. You may feel the presence of someone with you. Experiences vary tremendously and depend on the healing you need in the moment and the sense most available to you at that time.

With clairsentience, you may feel emotions like grief, shame, sadness, anger, worry, anxiety, fear, jealousy, guilt or derivatives of those emotions, which could suddenly appear with no obvious cause. The emotion can be strong and even cause an emotional reaction like crying or it may be gentle and mild, almost as if it belonged to someone else. Any sensation goes, so don't judge, just allow.

If the sensation is moving or changing, this is a sign of healing. That's what we want! As discussed earlier, energy that can't move leads to imbalance and disease and will feel stuck, without movement. On the other hand, sensations that shift in character, intensity or location freely change and allow the opportunity for healing.

One of my clients says she occasionally feels someone sitting on the side of her bed while she falls asleep. At first, this feeling scared her, but now it brings a sense of peace. Why does her intuition share this information? I advised my client to notice the emotions around the moment in question, to get further information (in this example, when she senses someone sitting on her bed). At bedtime, does my client need a feeling of protection? Does she feel lonely? Does she need to learn to work with her intuition without fear? When gaining insight into your own intuitive perceptions, use whatever comes to mind to deeply understand and leverage the information you receive.

I'm often asked how to know the difference between an energetic feeling and a physical feeling that warrants checking by a doctor. Often, this happens when a person already feels anxious about illness and sensations in the body. My guidance is this: if a sensation moves or changes, it is likely energy. Physical pain from a physical problem tends to be in the same location and generally of similar intensity. If you ever have concerns about your health, my advice is to get checked by your doctor, so you can feel confident the issue needing attention is not an immediate physical need, but rather an energetic one. That leaves you free to explore energy and sensations in your body without reservation.

> **Fundamental principle:** If a sensation moves and changes, it is likely energy. If it's in the same location and does not change, it could be a physical symptom.

Sense of Knowing: Claircognizance

The intuitive sense of knowing does not match a physical sense and can be more difficult to conceptualize. Britannica defines the intuitive sense of knowing as "having the ability to know or understand things without any proof or evidence." It is a deep sense of certainty or knowledge, without conscious reasoning or thought.

This is a powerful intuitive sense because you can tap into a greater universal pool of knowledge than what you may have read or studied personally. An example of this sense would be knowing a particular path is the right one. "I just feel this is the right house for us to purchase." For a food sensitivity patient, a weekend eating too many sweets may lead way to the following clarity: "Sugar is the cause of my inflammation symptoms."

In healing sessions using the intuitive sense of knowing, I may be drawn to a particular emotion relating to a symptom. I may have a sudden awareness of a parent's role in the illness of the client. This form of knowing, which can't be explained by any other information or source, guides me toward unresolved energy that requires healing.

Information perceived by claircognizance is incredibly useful, but it can be easy to believe your mind is simply making things up. The more you use this sense, the more you realize it is true information, not creations from your mind. As with all intuitive senses, just allow and notice what arises without judgment.

Sense of Hearing: Clairaudience

The intuitive sense of hearing allows you to hear intuitive information in your mind, rather than with your ears. Someone's voice, words, dishes shattering or an affirmation are all common ways the physical sense of hearing can bring information to your awareness. Alternatively, with the intuitive version, you hear words or sounds that are not spoken or have no physical origin.

For example, in a client session, I may hear with clairaudience, "I never do anything right," or "I'm afraid of him," or "I don't feel safe." As the healer, I receive this extrasensory information through words to help focus on the root disturbance in the body. It is typical for the mind to focus on a particular event, such as a traumatic memory, rather than seeing the broader patterns that influence how we perceive and navigate everyday life. That's why an outside perspective is so helpful. Paired with intuitive information, the intuitive healer can identify dysfunctional patterns that are so ingrained they're hidden from the client's awareness.

Use clairaudience in your own life to uncover energetic blockages your conscious mind may not be aware of. The perceptions you receive highlight experiences and beliefs that need healing, bringing awareness to symptoms and their root causes.

Awareness can be up to 80% of the solution to healing a pattern. Often, just knowing is enough to align focus to a more positive outcome, allowing it to come into your life. When awareness is present, your intuition can share the positive attributes you need, imprinting positive thoughts such as, "I am safe and protected." Aligning with new thought patterns can bring tremendous change to the function of your physical body, as well as your mindset and mood.

Sense of Sight: Clairvoyance

The intuitive sense of sight is dramatically described in the movies as someone looking into a crystal ball and seeing visions. Rest assured it can be much more practical than that. This sense can be disturbing if it's active at too early an age (children seeing people in their bedrooms, for instance).

This sense doesn't have to be disturbing or anxiety-producing. Subtle information is common and useful. Seeing a loved one's face, an image of your childhood bedroom, flashing back to an image of your high school class where you had to give a presentation are all common ways information can be brought by the sense of sight.

In healing sessions with clients, I often see mist, fog or a tangle of energy. I may also use tools to remove disruptive energy from the body. Seeing colors or energy formations around people are other ways your intuitive sense of sight can share information.

The intuitive sense of sight doesn't have to be uncomfortable. I had a teacher and mentor who found it disturbing to see actual body parts, so she asked for information to be revealed to her in sketch form, like the images in a high-school health book. Her intuitive sense adjusted to accommodate her wishes. Intuitive sense can be subtle and supportive, guiding your focus to life areas that need healing attention and providing tools to repair the imbalances.

Sense of Taste and Smell: Clairgustance and Clairolfaction

Intuitive senses of taste and smell include information received through your senses, not tied to physical stimuli. You may smell your grandmother's perfume, gasoline from a car accident, your elementary school classroom, or the fresh-baked bread your mom used to make, even though the smells are not physically present.

These smells orient your mind to energy that needs to come to awareness for healing, either to clear energy about a traumatic time in your life or bring in positive energy from a pleasant time. Both methods bring healing in different ways with different focus. Studies show that removing negative energy from the body focuses directed energy with precision for significant healing. Focusing on bringing in positive energy provides a different energetic effect. Lynne McTaggart reviews relevant research on the differences of the healer's focus in her book, *Living with Intention.*

I feel both clairgustance and clairolfaction are important in the healing process and I use both in healing sessions with my clients. These intuitive senses are a unique way to convey information. When you receive this sort of intuitive input, ask what is being brought to your awareness, especially if it isn't immediately obvious.

How to Listen to Your Body

Now that you know different ways intuitive information can come to awareness to share needed information, it's time to learn how to be open to receive for yourself. Receiving intuitive information requires a calm and quiet nervous system and mind to tune into the stream of information already coming to you. Let's specifically talk about how to do this.

You don't need to learn specific skills to listen to your body. In fact, you just need to *unlearn.* Children are born knowing how to be open and receptive with a quiet mind. They exist this way by default after birth. Their mind is quiet, not trapped in a constant stream of thoughts, which is typical for most adults. We all need to get back to the state we were born in!

There's a quick process for doing this. Some people immediately connect to energy, sensation or emotion in their body. For others, the process requires practice, so if it doesn't easily flow for you, don't give up the first time you try. Within a couple of weeks, most people notice major shifts. You can do this!

Step 1: Get Into the Body and Out of the Head

The first step is to quiet the mind and just be present—easier said than done, I know. My clients and I get frustrated when that pesky mind won't quiet. But just like anything else in life, it needs a little practice. This is a learned skill or rather, recovery of an innate skill you had at birth.

Get settled in a comfortable chair. Sit upright or you may fall asleep (trust me on this). Good lines of energy help you be awake and quiet without falling asleep. Don't lean back or slouch. You can sit cross-legged on the floor, upright on your bed with back supported, on the couch, at a desk or whatever works for you. Find a place where you can be supported and comfortable. If you're in a chair, your feet don't need to touch the floor, but it may help. Experiment to see what works best.

When you're comfortable, place a hand on your belly and a hand over your heart. This is optional but really helps you connect and focus on your body.

Now, imagine a shining light at the top of your head. It shines brightly in all directions. Focus on that light as it travels down through your head, throat and into your heart. Use your hand to help connect your awareness to your body, feeling your hand's presence on your heart or belly, drawing attention away from your head. Continue to see this light. Your mind should be quieting. If needed, notice your breath to help connect more deeply to your body.

Feel the sensation of the cool breath coming into your body, your chest rising and your belly filling. As you exhale, feel the release of the air. Sit for a moment and feel your mind being quiet and your focus directed in the present moment in the body.

Step 2: Open to Receive

Now that you're sitting in present awareness and focused on the body, what do you feel or sense? Do you feel an emotion, tightness, burning or something else? A person or a memory may flash in your mind. You may feel a sensation in your body. Whatever comes up, be open to receiving it. Sit quietly just listening in the moment, being with the body. If your mind wanders and starts focusing elsewhere, gently bring it back by refocusing on the breath, heart or belly.

Be open to receiving any information that can help you. I call this being open to receive, like a dish antenna waiting for signals from outer space. The perfect information will come to you at the perfect time. Do not despair if you don't sense anything. Just keep showing up and getting into the desired state. As you practice, your mind will become quieter, enabling more clarity and a greater ability to intuitively sense.

Step 3: Ground Down

At the conclusion of this exercise, bring focus back to the body and into the feet, connecting with the ground. It might help to visualize roots coming out of your feet connecting firmly into the ground. Do whatever feels best, making sure you visualize your energy coming down and connecting to the ground before you come back to the room into normal awareness.

With practice, this process of opening to receive and sensing becomes automatic. The power of this process comes from quieting your mind to bring awareness through intuition. Notice information that can help shift your perspective. In some cases, all you need to heal an energy blockage, emotional energy or limiting belief is simply awareness of it. Typically, 80% of the solution lies in awareness, but sometimes it can be one hundred percent! Just holding a sensation and allowing it to be there rather than resisting it, for example tightness in the chest or swirling in the stomach, typically results in a shift within thirty seconds. The sensation will somehow change; just stay with it. We will talk more about how to move energy in the coming chapters.

There is one other fundamental fact to realize: energy can shift if you simply create the space. If you open to receive, listen, and give permission for energy to move (for your system to release it), energy can move without you sensing it at all! How awesome is that? Yes, just by creating space for healing, it can happen. So don't despair or throw in the towel if you don't sense anything. Each person has a different process. Trust that the one you are experiencing is the perfect process for you!

I promise you will feel better with a calmer mind and more centered energy. With practice, you will sense more. Intuition is like any other skill in life: the more you practice, the easier it becomes. The more you calm your mind, the more automatic it becomes to tap into intuition. Give your system the opportunity to open to receive, once per day for a couple of weeks to help the process flow automatically.

Chapter 7: How to Rock Your Energy Health

Before we dig into moving energy, it's important to understand factors that influence your energy field. Awareness can suddenly bring past and present healing opportunities into focus for resolution. Healing opportunities from your past may shine like beacons for you to release energy that has kept you stuck in old patterns.

You've likely felt the drain of negative energy but thought you were just tired. This is a feeling worth noticing and doing something about. Let's explore this in more detail.

Energetic Boundaries

One cool crisp Monday morning, I woke up excited, on top of my game. I jumped out of bed, exercised, and made healthy lunches for the week. It was go time. I was driving to work, excited about the day, when I got a call from a stressed friend.

She was worried about her son's trouble focusing at school. He was falling behind in his schoolwork. At the same time, her husband was juggling a difficult job change. I offered needed support and a sympathetic ear. After the call, my mood had dropped from a ten to a seven.

This is a simple example of the power of energy. If you have a friend or family member who is struggling or routinely negative, it will affect you, especially if you spend substantial time around them. Your ability to protect yourself from their negative energy will govern how much time you can handle around them. Usually less is better. Sometimes people are unavoidable, for instance, a boss or family member. If this is your situation, you must learn how to strengthen your energetic boundaries.

Energetic boundaries are places where your energy stops and someone else's starts. There's a protective energy field at the boundary of your energy system, but it can weaken with illness, stress and unprocessed emotion. If you must put others' needs before your own, be hypervigilant to avoid obligation or power imbalances. Unbalanced situations can easily cause energy disruptions in the body.

If you're subconsciously afraid of disapproval, making a mistake or feeling overly responsible, your boundaries will be more at risk for weakness. When boundaries weaken, confusion grows, and the subconscious mind may not be clear where various energies rightly belong. If you've ever faced an angry family member and then also become angry, you've experienced weak energetic boundaries. Clearing and processing energy that no longer serves you will strengthen your energetic boundaries by removing energy blockages that affect the integrity of your energy field.

Young children and infants have weak energetic boundaries; they don't yet have a sense of self. If you had a volatile, angry or stressed parent, you likely took on some of that energy in early life without realizing it. Your nervous system may be in a stressed state as a result. Authority figures, parents, doctors, religious leaders, coaches, siblings, and teachers can all have strong influence, especially if they have difficult emotions or controlling personalities. As old environmental stress clears through energy work, your system will be stronger and more secure.

Environmental influences are not limited to people. Schools, religious groups, hospitals, teams, buildings, geopathic stress and even weather can affect your energy. Anything outside your own system is considered an environmental influence. By strengthening your energy system and removing boundary weaknesses, you increase your resilience to all environmental factors. Negativity is part of life, but it doesn't have to affect you.

Energy Vampires

Energy vampires are external influences affecting your energy. These people take energy from others instead of generating their own energy. They control others through shame, guilt or fear by criticizing, judging and threatening. They're takers, creating unstable situations they may not even be aware of. The victim of the energy vampire feels disempowered and self-doubt begins to grow. Soon, energy is weakened and in disarray, creating what I call an open door.

An open door is a weakness in your own energy field that leaves you vulnerable to attachment by others. Think of this as an unlocked door anyone can just walk in to steal and exploit your energy. Open doors are energetic wounds or disturbances from the past that can weaken your boundaries and leave you vulnerable. Think about a cut in your skin that leaves you at risk of infection. Once a scab forms, the cut is no longer a risk. The same is true for your energy. You must repair energetic wounds and injuries for boundaries to be strong and secure. Whatever originally caused the injury needs to be acknowledged so that the energy can be released.

Trauma, dysfunctional relationships and belief systems cause open doors. Abusers and volatile critical people who shame or belittle can create attachments that drain energy. Feelings of fear, shame and powerlessness are often at the root of these wounds, allowing unhealthy attachment. Think of a cord connecting you to this person. Once you clear the emotional wound that allowed the cord to connect, it falls away, leaving you free. You no longer give your energy away.

The result is a feeling of sovereignty, confidence and wholeness.

Anyone with significant control over your thoughts or actions can fall into this category. If you fear disapproval, there is likely an unhealthy attachment in place. Cords and attachments to a person who drains your energy can affect your current thoughts and actions. Once those connections are removed, you live freely on your own terms, without fear of what others might think. If it sounds freeing, it is!

Case Study: Energetic Connections

Kristine had severe digestive problems, was unable to tolerate many foods and had an extremely limited diet. She suffered with eczema and difficulty focusing on work. During childhood, her father traveled for significant stretches of time. Her mother was mentally unwell much of the time, unable to take charge. Kristine felt she had to be the adult rather than a child.

For a variety of reasons, she felt like a victim of her life and health. She developed deep frustration and feelings of powerlessness. In our sessions, we found deep energetic connections to her mother. She remembered feeling powerless against her mother's illness and her inability to be a strong parent. The relationship with her mother centered on powerlessness, affecting my client's digestive system and draining her personal power.

As part of Kristine's healing, we disconnected and repaired her connection with mom based on past traumatic memories of mom not being strong, often with no one else present to be in control and help my client feel safe. In this case, the mother's disempowerment caused disempowered energy in the child, creating blurred energy fields and violated energetic boundaries, leading to health dysfunction.

❧

Negative Energy and Grumpy People

If you've ever been affected by someone's negative mood, you've felt the impact of an environmental influence. It is possible to repel the negativity of others with strong boundaries. You can strengthen boundaries by clearing your energy field of stored emotion, destructive patterns and wounding. In short, you must be energetically whole.

That sounds like a tall order. Luckily, you don't have to achieve perfection. As you remove energy blockages, you strengthen your energy. When you feel better, your energy vibrates at a higher rate and begins to repel difficult situations and people. When you encounter negative energy, it bounces right off and doesn't affect you. That is the power of clearing blockages and building resilience.

The difficulty comes when someone with negative energy is in your everyday life. Perhaps you have a family member, good friend, coworker or boss who drags you down. After being with them, you usually feel worse than you did before. You often feel a victim in these situations, thinking you'd be happier if they were happier.

Be watchful for negative-energy people holding you back from your full energetic power. In these situations, you must dig deep to strengthen your system. Think of that person as an impetus to help you get stronger. They highlight an issue in your system that needs attention; it's up to you to take action to strengthen yourself and avoid triggering. In the coming chapters, you will learn to move energy to strengthen your boundaries.

Case Study: The Controlling Mother-In-Law

Janice dealt with chronic fatigue and pain. Her children also had health issues that demanded a lot of her energy and focus. One of her biggest stresses was her mother-in-law who often engaged her in power battles. She would arrive unannounced from out of town and reorganize various parts of Janice's home without permission.

The mother-in-law's inappropriate behavior carried over into interactions with Janice's friends and neighbors. She would call her grandchildren on the phone and undermine parental authority. My client felt victimized, out of control and deeply frustrated. When she tried to confront her mother-in-law or speak to her husband for support, excuses were made.

In our work together, we first unwound emotional abuse and deep rejection from Janice's parents and stepparents from her childhood. We healed the trauma of feeling out of control, unwanted and being deeply criticized as she moved from parent to parent. We repaired her heart energy, immune system, digestive system and treated chronic infections.

Finally, after much energy repair and release of past trauma, Janice was able to stand her ground with her mother-in-law. This allowed her to finally reclaim her personal power and hold crystal-clear boundaries with this difficult family member. In the process, her physical health and that of her children dramatically improved.

⤚

Grounding

Grounding is one of the steps of the open-to-receive process from the previous chapter. Let's more deeply explore how this relates to the body. According to *Oxford Languages,* grounding means to "connect (an electrical device) with the ground" or "place or lay (something) on the ground or hit the ground with it." Both definitions are relevant here.

Earlier I shared how your body has an energy system, electrical in nature. We discussed the common medical tests that measure the flow of electricity through the body. The body's energy system benefits from being electrically connected to the ground, just as you ground your house to protect your electronics from lightning strikes and electrical surges. Any electrician will share that grounding protects a system from a buildup or surge of energy. The same applies to your body. By grounding, you connect your body to the earth, discharging energy that isn't serving you and receiving positive energy from the ground.

There are two main components to grounding. First, you must be connected and aware of your body. This may sound simple, but humans have a tendency to get caught up and swept away by our mind and thoughts. If your mind is busy, it's nearly impossible to focus on your body and be present with it. Having your primary focus in the mind and away from the body works for short stretches, such as completing a big project at work. But if your focus is disconnected from your body for long periods, your energy remains ungrounded and vulnerable to imbalance.

Second, you must be connected to the physical world around you, in particular the earth, which has an energy called the Shuman resonance. The frequency of this energy is similar to the alpha brain wave state. Alpha waves are what you feel when you're in deep relaxation, meditation, or just entering/leaving a sleep state[15].

Hiking, gardening or enjoying nature connects you to the earth's marvelous, readily available energy source. Research shows that nature can calm your stress hormones and heart rate better than other activities like being outside at a playground or park. There really is something special about nature and its proven energy impact on the body[16].

Heart Armoring

The heart is your harmonizer and balancer, the strongest energy field in your body. It's no wonder then that heart energy disruptions are highly influential. When you have an experience that makes you think, "I never want to feel that way again," you most likely try to protect yourself by creating an emotional barrier. Such barriers are often completely hidden in the subconscious mind.

Beliefs such as "Female friends are judgmental" or "Men can't be trusted" or "I can't trust myself" create highly effective barriers that keep pain at bay. However, they also block joy. Those beliefs may have been true in your past, but they don't have to be true in your future. They limit your ability to feel good, attract positive experiences and connect with others in meaningful ways.

This energy dynamic in the heart is known in healing circles as a heart wall or heart armoring. Imagine this energy as a shield around the heart or a stone wall fortress, preventing the smooth flow of energy. These structures result from painful relationships, loss of loved ones, abuse, self-criticism, or other difficult circumstances.

In order for your heart to generate joy, which is instrumental to happiness, you must shed the traumas that created the heart armoring. This frees the heart to function in balance. Instead of storing and carrying negative emotions, the heart is free to generate joy and connect in deep, meaningful ways with others. These dynamics are not only about feeling good; this energy center plays a major role in the physical function of your immune system.

Medical research proves the link between how you feel and the function of your immune system: feeling good boosts your immune function and stress suppresses it[17,18]. Immune dysfunction plays a key role in chronic illness, including cancer, recurrent infection, autoimmune disease, allergic reactions and inflammatory diseases. By unburdening heart energy, you boost immune strength and balance. It can feel intimidating to do this work, but it's well worth the effort. The symptom shifts I see working with heart energy and the immune system are staggering. Unburdening the heart can be so powerful it's almost hard to believe.

Lifestyle Factors Impact Energy

News abounds about the importance of lifestyle factors such as diet, alcohol intake, physical activity and stress levels. What you eat, how you sleep and how you move matter in relation to your body's mental and physical health. It should come as no surprise that the same factors affect your energy.

When you do something that doesn't support your health, it creates stress in your body. If your body is well-rested, healthy and resilient, you recover quickly. Think of your college days when you stayed out until the wee hours of the morning, able to recover overnight. By the time you hit your forties or fifties, you probably have lost that ability to rebound so quickly. The body can function under suboptimal conditions, but it takes longer to recover and most importantly, it creates stress.

Eating hard-to-digest food and drinking alcohol place stress on your body that the liver must clear. Staying up late, cramming for an exam and working long hours to meet a work deadline cause stress. Remember, stress creates energy blockages in the body and, over time, affects your body's function. If your body is weakened or less resilient, stress drains your vitality and begins to cause symptoms. Over months and years, stressors build up, especially if you don't build in recovery time.

When it comes to biology, feelings of stress and overwhelm cause the sympathetic nervous system (the fight-or-flight response) to produce cortisol and adrenaline. In this state, your nervous system shunts rest-and-digest activities and instead mobilizes a stress response, including increasing your heart rate, directing blood to your limbs, turning off digestion and focusing resources to spring into action. Entering this state for a short time may not be a big deal. However, if you do it every day or multiple times a day, your nervous system will get stuck in that state, unable to slow down to carry out normal repair functions in the body.

When you're stuck in fight or flight, all spare energy is directed toward survival. A chronic ankle injury can become increasingly inflamed in a state of stress, as the body's repair mechanisms are compromised. With prolonged activation of the fight-or-flight response, your adrenal glands struggle to keep up with the demands of ongoing stress. The system becomes exhausted and suffers. Imbalances of hormones, digestion, mood and energy start to take hold. This lays the foundation for chronic illness.

So, lifestyle matters but how do you use this information? By choosing to lower lifestyle stress, you lower the total amount of stress your body must cope with. In doing so, your body heals and recovery starts. For example, I believe food sensitivities, allergies, and infections can heal. But to make this possible, you must decrease stress so your immune system can repair. Lifestyle factors are key in this process.

Other important lifestyle factors play roles in your health by adding energy to the system. Healthy food provides the nutrition your body needs. Deep, restorative sleep helps the body heal and repair. Relaxing activities and connection with loved ones bring joy into your life, helping you feel a sense of purpose and boosting your mood and energy levels. It may be tempting to ignore lifestyle factors, but your body deserves the benefit of decreased stress and increased resilience.

With all this talk about the importance of the mind, it would be natural to think that if you change your thoughts, you can change your reality. This is partially true. It's true that you create the world around you by focusing energy and attention. So, you may have assumed that if you don't want a particular symptom in your life, just pretend it doesn't exist.

This thinking has one big flaw: energy stored in your body can sabotage your ability to manifest a body free of symptoms. The mind is powerful; it creates amazing problems and solutions. However, the mind is just part of the story. Your body is a massive receptacle for stored energy, with complex processes, systems and tissues. Disruptive energy becomes stored not just in the mind, but also in the body.

> **Fundamental principle:** Denial doesn't work.

When you change your mind over time, you will indeed change your physiology, but stored energy must also leave the body in order to create health. As both the mind and body release energy blockages, physiology can quickly shift.

By just changing your mind without addressing stored energy in the physical body, you're at risk of creating denial patterns. I've tried this many times and it just doesn't work, plain and simple. A positive mindset is a powerful tool; however, it cannot negate the importance of avoiding foods, people and situations that create stress in your body until your physiology shifts. It's essential to honor your system's weaknesses until healing alters those needs. For instance, I believe food sensitivities can heal, but consuming foods that stress the body will only weaken it until healing occurs and the sensitivity resolves. We will revisit this idea in coming chapters.

Illness, Injury and Energy

Illnesses may seem random. You may suddenly catch a cold or find yourself with flu-like symptoms. It's never pleasant to feel unwell, but did you realize there can be an energetic gift in illness? Fever is the body's natural mechanism to fight infection. As the temperature rises, infectious agents like viruses and bacteria cannot survive and become more vulnerable to immune attack. In my experience and that of my clients, fever is a great way to burn off infections and with them, energy.

It is a well-known fact young children may reach new developmental milestones after an illness with fever. A child client of mine with recurrent molluscum infections spiked a fever the evening after her session. After a short illness, her skin infections finally found resolution and never returned.

The unpleasant symptoms of vomiting and diarrhea are one of the most effective ways to shift energy; they may also be the most miserable. I once worked deeply on fear in my own life. I did many energy sessions for myself, allowing information about my past to come to awareness. For six months or more, this was my primary focus. In frustration, I said to the universe, "I will do whatever I need to get rid of this fear in my body." I was tired of working with it!

The very next day, I seemingly caught a stomach bug. For twenty-four hours, I had vomiting and diarrhea, an incredibly rare occurrence for me. I was miserable. Within twenty-four hours, my symptoms vanished and no one else in my household got sick. This was highly suspicious because, with small children, usually every bug ran through the entire house. The beautiful gift was this: as my symptoms vanished, so did my fear. It was such a relief that this energy lessened in my life. Injury can similarly serve energy movement and free stuck energy to move.

One winter day several years ago, I was splitting wood on my property with our gas-powered wood splitter. It's always a judgment call on how big or little to split logs and where to split them. Keep in mind, big oak trees that die on our property can be massive, over two feet in diameter. I was splitting with a helper, log after log. One of us put the log on the splitter and the other worked the lever. I was on lever duty and maybe because I was bored, I began judging my helper. He put the log on the track and I thought, *It's not going to split that way because of the knot.* Then a few logs later, *that needs to be split again,* and *that one doesn't need to be split.*

I didn't say any of this out loud, but it didn't matter. I recognized that I was judging, which amused me. Within two minutes, as I rolled the next piece of wood toward the splitter, a massive log (probably 300 pounds) slipped when I lost my grip; I fell and jammed my finger. It was the finger related to the pericardium meridian governing relationships with others and openness. A coincidence? I believe the injury helped my body release stored judgment energy, freeing me from unhealthy patterns from my past.

So, this begs the question: do we have to get sick or injured to shift energy? I've studied this question deeply over the years. In my experience, the answer is definitely no. However, sometimes we're unable to face energy locked in the physical body. Perhaps it's too big, too scary or otherwise inaccessible. You may not know it exists or you can't "see" it. If you haven't found a way to move the energy but your system is ready to be free of it, illness or injury can force it to move.

Chapter 8: The Prism of Creation

What is the purpose of the hardships you experience? I am often asked this question, especially when significant health challenges cause deep pain and frustration. As stated earlier, I believe symptoms are the body's way of getting your attention. I find that once you identify and heal the underlying energetic root cause of symptoms, they really do go away! Even the most stubborn infections, chronic pain or cancer can disappear once the energy is resolved. Your symptoms are like flashlights shining awareness on your life experiences.

In my experience, everyone has several big energy themes to explore and master. You can recognize them because they're challenging to conquer and they come up again and again. You may feel you're stuck in the same movie day in and day out. However, once you master the root energies of those experiences, your life will shift, and the pattern will change.

Such freedom paves the way for joy and feeling well. Energy healing is the perfect tool to address the root cause of those threads—often from your childhood or other deeply formative experiences—moving them out with more speed and ease than simply learning from experience by itself.

We've talked about how your mind and energy interpret life events through the five senses, the filter of everything you experience. I call this process the prism of creation. Quantum physics proves the concept of universal energy to constantly create reality. Universal energy travels through your consciousness to manifest your experiences. It influences what you create. No, you don't consciously choose what you create or you would never have difficulties or discomfort! Your higher self and energy choose. If you understand this, you can leverage universal energy for healing and growth.

Think of creation ability as a big crystal with many facets. Energy comes down into the crystal, perhaps with color, cloudiness, fogginess or other blockages. As you clear your consciousness and negative experiences or belief systems, the crystal clears. It directs incoming energy into precise projection. With each healing and cleansing of the energy field you clear the prism of creation to create more joy and ease.

According to the law of attraction, you attract experiences compatible with your current vibration. So, if you feel unsafe in your surroundings, you will attract experiences that help you feel unsafe to process and conquer fear. When the fear is gone, you feel safe. Then you can attract experiences that feel safe in your world. This is the path of true healing.

Here's an example: I have food sensitivities that cause discomfort, making me feel that eating is unsafe. Each time I eat, I'm cautious to avoid foods that make me feel bad. This continuous focus and repetition of problem foods further reinforces the idea that food isn't safe and causes discomfort (a vicious cycle). The cycle can strengthen over time if left unchecked, allowing food sensitivities to continue and worsen because my focus is directed at the problem.

On the other hand, if I can heal my perception of food as unsafe, and begin to view it as safe and nourishing, my food sensitivities will heal. I will attract experiences that address my physiological issues, such as supplements, diets and medical treatments. As fear dissipates and a sense of safety emerges, my body functions can normalize. I can then enjoy nourishing foods without fear of discomfort. This heals the root cause of food dysfunction, which can be expanded and applied to other situations in health and life.

In my practice, there is always a significant thread of energy (or two or three) underlying chronic illness. The trick to finding true healing is to unwind the energy to allow the body to heal.

There is a spiritual journey and lesson in your experiences, which leads to my favorite advice about difficulty. Any time you feel bewildered, frustrated or stuck, ask this simple question: "What do I need to learn for this situation to resolve?"

Find a place to sit without interruption. Take a few centering breaths, close your eyes and ask what you need to learn. Then open to allow information to bubble into awareness. You may receive guidance immediately, a few hours later or in the coming days. This guidance can come in a variety of forms including intuition, sudden inspiration, dramatic change or a new solution opening for you. Just open to allow and you will likely receive clarity about the next step to take.

This simple question will reorient your out-of-control feeling to one of empowerment and confidence to create positive change. You will be able to act and understand instead of feeling stagnant, frustrated or overwhelmed. Asking what you need to learn from a situation also opens the door for guidance, creating a mode of listening and receiving, rather than desperately trying to fix or remedy a situation yourself. Openness allows solutions to come to you, solutions that can change everything: healers, supplements, knowledge, relationships, support.

My husband and I were in the process of deciding whether to buy an office building. It was a beautiful old building more than 100 years old with lots of charm and great energy. The commute was just over ten minutes from our home, which sounded great compared to the 25-minute commute I'd had for six years. The building seemed perfect, until the home inspection.

The inspector's report indicated the foundation and roof rafters needed significant work. We could see that a corner of the foundation was crumbling and the roof rafters were significantly bowed. The back porch was out of code, a "death trap" according to the inspector.

Suffice it to say, the building needed significant investment. The sellers completely dismissed the findings from the home inspection and basically said take it or leave it. I couldn't believe they would deny such obvious findings. After much consideration, we walked away from the deal; it was just too much for us to deal with.

Fast forward six months: the house was still on the market. It still felt like the best location for my business. We reengaged and asked the sellers if we could visit the property with an engineer to get a quote for the needed work. Even though our agent continued to inquire with their agent, they didn't respond. I was so frustrated. I spent several days feeling unsettled. One day as I was driving, I asked, "What do I need to learn for this situation to resolve?"

Frustration bubbled up and I realized I was angry because they were acting differently than I expected. Sure, that was their prerogative. As I held that thought, I suddenly flashed back to childhood. I felt an old frustration that my desires weren't my parents' priority. I allowed myself to feel that frustration, seeing myself as a young child venting anger. As I drove home, my mood improved. The very next day, we got word that the sellers agreed to let us into the building to get the needed quote. My emotional release of frustration allowed the situation to shift and progress. And yes, the building is now the lovely home of my business.

This approach is powerful. Many clients have brought a stuck situation to resolution by asking this question. Try it! When you feel stuck or uncomfortable, simply follow the steps described above and ask, "What do I need to learn for this situation to resolve?"

I have seen dramatic shifts occur when you identify and work through difficulties caused by energy. This includes sudden job offers, an unexpected influx of money to improve finances, troubled relationships that suddenly shift and the perfect health treatment to suddenly appear. It's amazingly powerful, especially when you feel powerless. Remember that every life experience is there for a reason. It's your job to be open to healing stuck energy to move on to a life filled with more ease and joy.

This brings us to a lesson from cultures throughout the world: life is your mirror. When an experience comes to you or you see an unpleasant trait in someone else, is there a similar pattern you are failing to see in yourself? If I complain that my kids don't listen to me, what exists in me allowing the trigger? Do I not listen to myself or others? Do I need to value myself for others to listen to me? What do I need to know for the situation to shift?

A few years ago, one of my children wanted nothing to do with me. I'm not exaggerating; it was a mom's worst nightmare. One day he was at his computer playing games and I asked how he was doing. "Fine," my fourteen-year-old mumbled, not looking up and continuing his game. I tried another conversation starter, "Anything new at school?" "No," he mumbled again. And so it went. Getting any kind of meaningful response was nearly impossible. This continued for a couple of months. I was hurt. "What did I do to deserve this?" I wondered.

My mind knew this was probably a normal developmental teenage milestone en route to independence, but it seemed quite extreme. My emotions got the better of me and I felt angry, anxious and hurt. It became obvious this wouldn't resolve on its own. I felt invisible and decided to offer myself the same advice I give clients.

As I pondered the problem, I realized that part of me needed him to connect with me. Suddenly, a whole pile of emotion flooded my awareness, especially fears of him not needing me. I immediately flashed back to my own childhood. I felt anxious when my parents traveled out of the country, leaving us at home. Worried that something would happen to them, I calculated when they would arrive at their destination so I could relax, knowing they were safe when I didn't hear bad news. I remembered my son's intense separation anxiety as a young child and my feelings of guilt when I had to leave him. I worked on this in one session, simply recognizing and allowing all that energy to clear. I felt much lighter after this.

The next day, I felt a definite sense of freedom. I didn't care if he wanted to talk to me or not. I was okay with neutrality, confident that his reluctance to talk was just a phase he was going through. The very next day, he started a conversation with me! I was amazed how quickly this work completely shifted the situation. My son's attitude toward me triggered subconscious anxiety related to my parenting and being parented so that I could work through these patterns. Once the anxiety was gone, there was freedom. We have been happily connecting ever since.

It's possible for you to look at illness in a new way. Energy comes in, moves through the prism of creation and the filter of your consciousness and manifests your reality. You can view life as this prism of creation, understanding how you have been influenced by stored emotions, past experiences and belief systems. Another way to think of this is a pair of sunglasses. The lenses don't change what you see, but they color the image. Perhaps your past creates a rosy hue around life or perhaps a smoky one. Either way, your view of the world is shaped to match your past experiences and belief systems.

More importantly, shading or filtering affects universal energy coming into your body. Energy comes in, passes through lenses or filters and affects what you create. In your creative center, energy is filtered by your consciousness: the collection of your belief systems, stored emotion and how you view the world. These filters help you create experiences to resolve energies that no longer serve you.

If you feel fearful, you will attract experiences to help you work through the fear. When it comes to your health, if you feel anxious about your body being unwell, you will create negative experiences until that anxiety resolves and you deeply own the belief that your body can heal.

If you have energy from past unwell experiences stored in your body, you will feel unwell until that energy is released. In effect, if you create illness, you misdirect creative energy through a filter of illness. In this example, you create what you don't want.

Luckily there's a way to change misdirection by working with your energy system. If you change the prism, you project health instead of illness.

Is something hiding in your prism that may be projecting and creating health symptoms? In the following chapters you will discover key experiences that may affect your prism and how to heal them to create health.

Part II. The Time to Heal Is Now

Chapter 9: Practical and Simple Processes for Healing

You may assume that healing must be hard, but that doesn't have to be the case. Healing can be spontaneous, gentle and powerful. You don't have to relive trauma or feel years of suppressed emotion from your past to find relief. Physical symptoms can indeed heal, including those that doctors don't know how to address. Energy healing gives you the tools to do just that.

It is widely acknowledged that energy follows intention. Energy healing brings attention to something that needs to heal and creates change using focused intention. In the coming chapters, you will learn simple, powerful ways to heal your body's energy. Focused intention can come through a healer or yourself. It doesn't matter. In the interactive session that follows, you will use a combination of your energy and mine to create results you can feel. Before we begin our interactive session, let's review some helpful background information to empower you with new skills and knowledge.

Process Sensations in the Body: The EMOT Process

EMOT (Energy Move Out Technique) is a simple effective process to help move energy blockages in the body. You can release energy blockages by yourself, without any specialized training. (Yes, you can do this!) I developed this simple process to help clients move energy efficiently and easily. Moving energy can be easy without requiring a lot of knowledge. I'll teach you a simple process to follow that can bring immediate relief.

Remember, energy blockages are stresses of any kind lodged in the body's energy field. All you need to do is find them, allow them to be there and help them move out. Often, you don't need to know where it is or what it is; you just need to work with whatever you feel: a feeling, sensation, memory or something else. The power of the process lies in its simplicity and flexibility.

The EMOT process is simple and well worth your time. It's not magic, although it may seem like it. All steps are explained by quantum physics and consciousness research. Let's dive into this three-step process.

1. **Recognize.** Be aware of what is happening in your body. Recognize how you feel in this moment. Focus inward and take a few centering breaths, clear and quiet your mind and bring your focus into your chest or belly. Be open to receive. Revisit the process described in more detail in chapter six if needed. As you get into the present moment with your body, notice what comes to your awareness. Stillness will allow you to cut through the noise to feel intuitive information.

   You may notice an emotion, sensation, memory, person or sometimes nothing. If you sense an emotion but aren't sure how to label it, use the emotion encyclopedia in Appendix C for inspiration. This step is helpful but not required. If you feel a body sensation such as tightness in the chest, butterflies in the stomach or pain in a particular place, simply notice it. If someone's face pops into your mind, hold it. If a concern about the future comes up, notice it. Any information is useful; simply open to receive without judgment or the urge to make sense of the information. Try to keep your mind quiet, minimizing thought as much as possible.

Don't be discouraged if something comes up that you thought was behind you, even something you've worked on many times before. It's okay! An aspect of it still exists and is ready to be released. Its resurfacing can help create the freedom you've been seeking.

2. **Allow/feel.** You've recognized energy ready to shift. Give it permission to be there. Often, we distract ourselves or rationalize emotions away with our thoughts. Don't judge, distract or deny your feelings, sensations or memories. Even if you've worked on this energy before, perhaps a different aspect of it is bound in your body, ready to be released. Connect with what you feel; allow it to be there without judgment and without involving the mind. Sit with the emotion or sensation until you notice a change. This process doesn't take long. Usually, the energy changes within 15 to 45 seconds and you notice either a change or a release. Continue to hold for a few minutes. It may not be gone completely in this amount of time, but it will likely shift.

You may notice energy changing to a different location, emotion or intensity. Trust the process and know that all changes come in the way that best supports your system. Rest assured that any change is a sign of movement and progress. It's important to note you don't need to express your emotion to anyone, even if it involves others. You simply need to connect with the energy and feel it.

3. **Permission to leave.** Allow the energy to become a thing of the past! Past energy you've held for a long time can be difficult to release even if your mind is one hundred percent on board. If emotion or energy feels stuck, say out loud to yourself, "I give permission for this energy to leave. Thank you, energy, for

serving me. I no longer need you. I release all connections to you."

Repeat this statement two or three times, more if necessary. Feel free to add force, determination and resolve to your words. Say it like you mean it! If you no longer feel the energy, the process is complete. If you still sense incompleteness, take a break and proceed to the next section about what to do if energy feels stuck.

It's common to worry that emotional energy will overpower you, that it will never leave if you allow yourself to feel it. This couldn't be further from the truth. Feeling difficult emotion isn't pleasant, but in my experience, it begins to shift within just 30 to 45 seconds. As you first connect to your feelings, you may feel intense emotion. If you remain connected to the feeling, it will shift in intensity, shift into another emotion or release. The change you feel indicates energy movement. Movement, even if it feels unpleasant, is a sign of healing. By contrast, feeling stuck is a sign of stagnation. Energy leaves when you process it.

When you don't allow emotion, you lock it in your body, stored as suppressed energy. Your conscious mind will likely forget about it (out of sight, out of mind), but it will remain there, disrupting your body functions.

When a wave of emotion comes in, allow it to move and it will wash out, like water returning to the sea. The emotional energy in the body will similarly wash in and leave again if allowed to process. On the other hand, if you try to hold and contain the wave, the water will be stored. In summary, holding or suppressing equals storage. Allowing or expressing equals release.

This doesn't mean you have to break down in tears in the middle of a meeting when someone criticizes you. Luckily, you can put emotions on a back burner if they come up inconveniently. There are times when it isn't possible to work with energy, such as when you're at work or when you have to be "on" and engaged with others. The important thing is to return to the energy for complete processing in order to avoid an energy blockage. I find that a quick quiet moment at home, driving or before bed, usually does the trick. Practiced as needed, EMOT is a way to process difficult emotions without creating energy blockages and can lead to long-term health.

When Energy Feels Stuck

There are times when energy is stubborn and resists release. Here are a few time-tested tips to get it moving.

Revisit permissions. Reread the permission statements above. Say them with force and mean them. Reaffirm why you're ready to embrace a new way of living. Realize you indeed have the power to move energy. We all do. Give yourself permission to own this power.

Stand firm. Remember this important fact: if the energy comes to your awareness, you have the power to shift it. This is true even if you don't believe it! Use this knowledge to boost your confidence. If you couldn't shift it, it would stay hidden. Reassure yourself that you have the power to do it and that the process works. Hold the energy or stuck feeling and ask what you need to know to resolve it. Open to memories, emotions, people and any information that may come to awareness. Do you feel inadequate? Do you feel unsafe? Do you believe that healing must be hard? Is a hidden part of you afraid to heal? Notice any of these that feel true and give them permission to leave. Remember, those thoughts aren't true; they're just stories in your mind.

Move your body. Deep breathing, moving your spine or taking a walk can help move energy. Take a few deep breaths to move your diaphragm to allow internal energy to shift. Stand and do simple side stretches or bend over to move your circulation. Take a five-to-ten-minute walk to create movement in your body. Often, these simple activities create gentle movement that brings relief from stuck energy.

Energy visualization. Picture energy cleansing your energy field. Visualize white light coming into your head, washing through your body like a river, washing away energy that isn't serving you. Start at the head and imagine each cell lighting up with energy. Move to the neck, down the shoulders and arms, through the chest, belly, pelvis, hips and down the legs into the ground. Now bring the light from the ground up the entire body and see it illuminated. See the light inside your cells as you let go of energy that isn't serving you.

Take a break. If you need a break, take a short walk, clear your mind and try again later. As may happen with movement, you may find that a break allows the energy to shift without further action from you.

Ask for help. The first place to ask for help is your higher power. Universal consciousness, Source, God, Mother Nature, Divine, whatever aligns with your beliefs—ask for help and guidance. Asking for help can align all parts of you with healing. It's easy to do. Just ask in the most perfect way for you: prayer, meditation, visualization or any other method that works.

Get professional help. If you try everything in your power to shift energy blockages and you still feel stuck, it's time to reach out for help. Find a trusted healer or spiritual teacher whose energy is aligned with yours and ask for assistance. In my personal experience, sometimes you just need community.

When to Interrupt, When to Allow

With energy and emotional blockages, it's important to know when to interrupt negativity and when to allow it. One of the most common questions clients ask is how to handle negativity when it comes up in day-to-day experience. There are two primary ways negativity surfaces in your daily life: thoughts and emotions.

Let's start with negative thinking, an easy clear-cut case. Remember that thoughts create emotions. Always interrupt negative thinking. It never serves you. Both conscious and subconscious negative thoughts create emotion, including self-doubt, fear, anxiety, suffering, envy and powerlessness.

If you catch yourself with thoughts that don't feel good, notice them and redirect your mind. Remember, negative thoughts generate negative emotion and need to be redirected, including overthinking, self-criticism, anxiety and worry. Thought loops serve no purpose for higher good and healing; they need to leave. When you interrupt them, you immediately stop the flow of negative emotion. You get instant relief! This is a powerful way to shift how you feel.

It helps to first understand that your thoughts are not always true: they're creations of your mind. When a thought creates discomfort, ask yourself if it's really true. Byron Katie's *The Work* is founded on this process. As you become aware of and notice your thoughts, it will get easier and quicker to spot negative thinking.

Negative emotions, on the other hand, require a different approach. When an emotion comes up that isn't overwhelming, allow it to be there. Feel it and respond to it. For example, to handle frustration about not finding your keys in the morning, feel the frustration. This isn't hard to process because the emotion is manageable. Feel it and choose a response to move forward. Use this process freely with minor emotional triggers.

When emotional energy is overwhelming or creates paralyzing confusion, you may need additional tools. The EMOT process is the simplest and most effective method I've found to move emotional energy. If you're present with your emotion without thought, it can move.

Most of us experience times where we are resistant to releasing energy. When this happens, the permission step will help dissolve those anchors. But remember, your free will trumps all. If there's a part of you that doesn't want to let go, it must be explored before the energy can leave.

Be gentle with yourself throughout this journey. Energy blockages and negative conditioning are normal processes. You were likely conditioned to think certain ways in childhood. Your awareness brought the pattern to your attention because it no longer aligns with who you want to be. You're ready to up your game. By interrupting a negative thought pattern or releasing emotional energy, you instantly increase your vibration and feel better. Always do this with compassion.

What to Expect and What You Will Feel

When energy blockages are eliminated, you will feel lighter, less stressed and more peaceful. You'll be more resilient to stress of all kinds and feel expanded, like you can breathe deeper. There may be a sense of lightness as if a weight has been lifted from your shoulders. Clients most commonly report these feelings when energy blockages begin to move out. They also report better sleep and a reduction in symptoms. Let's discuss a few specifics that may apply to you.

As the stress axis downregulates and your nervous system goes from fight-or-flight mode to rest-and-digest mode, you may feel tired. The stillness you feel after the body has been overactive can feel like fatigue. This is a healthy recalibration and is completely normal. Within 24-48 hours, fatigue from energy shifting will pass without incident. You may notice a sudden change in the foods you want to eat. You may feel you're fighting off a mild illness or experience an aggravation of past pain as the body works through energetic change. You may have a headache for a few hours, typically in the forehead, though this is less common.

These responses to energy healing are all transient and short-lived, generally gone within 24-48 hours as mentioned above. The most important thing you can do is give yourself downtime. Relax, take a hot bath, go to bed early and skip social events to give yourself extra space for your body to shift.

Emotionally, you may feel agitated. If you shifted anxious energy or felt unsafe from your past, your body may continue to recognize ways you feel unsafe in present life. This doesn't mean the healing didn't work or didn't take hold; rather, it means your body is going deeper now that a big roadblock is out of the way. Shifting residual energy usually comes to your awareness and shifts out easily without need for intervention if you just allow the emotion to move through you.

Let yourself connect with and feel any emotion that surfaces, knowing you're going deeper. It's like sweeping up dust left on the floor after a big move. One of the most frequent questions I get after sessions is whether residual emotion means the work didn't hold. The answer is absolutely no. Once an energy blockage is cleared, it's gone forever. There's no way for the initial energy to return. You may connect with additional energy in your body related to the initial balance; this simply presents another opportunity for healing. I often tell clients that I clear the major blockages, allowing their system to continue cleaning house and shifting the additional energy that becomes visible. Another analogy is the layers of an onion: once the outer layer is cleared, the next layer is ready for healing.

Mentally, your mind will feel quieter. It will feel downregulated, churning less and being able to exist in a quieter, easier present-moment state. Meditation may become possible now when it wasn't in the past. Ruminating is likely to decrease in intensity, frequency or both. You may no longer feel like your mind is spinning.

As the noise in mind and body decreases, your mind becomes quieter and more present. This is freeing and calming. You are likely to feel peaceful and focused. Remember this shift is a massive benefit to your system because the mind creates emotion. With a quieter mind, there will be fewer negative thoughts to generate difficult emotion.

Spiritually, you will feel that clarity and intuition will be more accessible. You'll feel more supported and whole. With the ability to connect to this large part of yourself, you'll no longer feel alone or unsupported. You'll be able to rely on wisdom beyond your experience and be able to ask for guidance from your higher self. You may discover a new purpose, consider a job change or take up a new hobby. These changes are exciting signs of expansion!

As you release your connection to old energy blockages and outdated ways of looking at life through the lens of stress and trauma, you may feel disoriented. It may seem as though the world is shifting beneath your feet, leaving you unsure of who you are anymore. This is a normal transient feeling as you let go of old patterns from your past that no longer define you. This feeling can last anywhere from a few hours to a few weeks, depending on the magnitude of your energy shift.

When everything feels new, it may be! Letting go of fear, anxiety, powerlessness and unworthiness lets you step into an entirely new experience, full of empowerment, confidence and abundance. This can be a big change; you're creating a new, higher vibration identity, letting go of old lower vibration identities from your past that no longer serve you. During this process, you may experience mild discomfort. If it happens to you, get grounded using the recommendations provided in Chapter 11. If at any point you feel significant confusion and disorientation, talk with your healthcare practitioner.

Triggering

Triggering can happen anytime, but it's especially common once you signal you're ready to commit to healing. Remember, triggering is a gift from your subconscious bringing awareness to part of you that is ready to heal. Even though it's typically unpleasant, triggering is a sign for you to clean house and process old energy that has been holding you back.

It's time to anchor a higher vibration in your life. You're here to have an impact. Congratulations! Few have the courage to embark on this journey, and even fewer achieve the rewards of a joy-filled, peaceful and healthy existence.

This is the payoff for your efforts. As you navigate each triggering experience, you'll feel lighter and more peaceful. Each time you feel triggered by a specific emotion, its intensity will diminish. Once the emotional backlog is gone, your difficult emotion will just be a flash in the pan, a quick healthy emotional response of appropriate magnitude.

Core Stressors: Energy Blockage Creators

The first step in the healing process is to understand the core stresses that typically create energy blockages throughout life. Below I list common life events that create unresolved energy. If you've encountered these experiences, ask if there is unresolved energy affecting you. Of course, you can have multiple accidents or injuries, ongoing abuse, multiple breakups or divorces. Any of these can happen more than once in the span of your life.

Open to allow your body to share areas that need focus, in a way that is perfect for you. Realize there are many opportunities in the average life for experiences that cause energy blockages. There's no way to cover them all here. (That is another book!) What I will share are the basics to get you started. Don't feel limited by this list. If, for instance, you spent weeks in a NICU after your birth and everyone feared for your survival, include that too.

I recommend having pen and paper handy to jot down impressions, memories and notes related to your life experiences. You can use this list to highlight areas that may hold unresolved energy which you can focus on in the upcoming interactive healing session.

Accidents or injuries. This includes car accidents, broken bones, concussions, brain injuries, falls, sports accidents and any other event when your body or mind was traumatized by an accident or injury. The emotional response to these events matters as much as the physical impact. For instance, don't discount a car accident if you weren't significantly injured but still felt traumatized. On the flip side, if a fall wasn't traumatic emotionally but physical effects lingered, consider listing them here.

Catastrophic event. House fires, earthquakes, hurricanes, wildfires, wildfire smoke, floods, tornados, storms, public incidents of violence or building collapses are a few examples of catastrophes that can displace or traumatize you at any age, including before birth. Consider any major catastrophe you or your family endured.

Abuse (verbal, physical, emotional or sexual), including attempted abuse. Abuse of any kind leaves marks on your energy. Emotional imprints of fear, shame, grief and anger are common. Physical effects can linger as well, including dysfunction in affected body parts or the inability to express yourself in the endocrine system (thyroid, reproductive and adrenal hormone systems).

Abuse, whether attempted one time or over a period of time creates an unsafe environment. If abuse occurred in childhood, include the fundamental failure of adults in your life to keep you safe. Abuse experienced in adulthood also applies, including spousal abuse, workplace abuse and other abuse of power. Look to these difficult experiences to identify energy blockages.

Remember this important fact: with energy healing, you do not need to re-experience the difficult emotions of those experiences to clear the energetic charge around them. When you remember an event, simply bring your focus there for healing and follow the EMOT process or highlight the experience in the interactive healing session that follows.

Addiction. Alcoholism, drug addiction, smoking, vaping, sugar, inability to regulate food intake, excessive shopping, hoarding, gambling, social media scrolling or any other addiction that significantly affects daily life and living conditions apply here. If you cannot control the activity, it is likely affecting your body chemistry, driven by energy blockages simmering beneath the surface.

Assault. Threatened assault and fights of any kind lead to energetic imbalance and can cause draining energetic connections with victimizers. From being pushed down on the playground to being victimized during a crime, assault leaves feelings of vulnerability and lack of safety. These events often create energy blockages that affect mental and physical health.

Birth of a child or new sibling. The birth of a baby can be exciting for the whole family, but even with excitement comes stress. A new baby requires a tremendous amount of care, diverting parents' focus. Anger, resentment and loss of love are typical feelings for young children upon the birth of siblings. Additional hardship is incurred if the new child has high needs. For parents, the immediate introduction of a new human brings lack of sleep, difficulty meeting their own needs, hormonal shifts in the family and other stresses. The adoption process creates energetic challenges as well, even if the process is smooth.

Breakup or divorce of parents or your own relationships. Divorce is a major adverse childhood event for good reason: everything changes. If the home was volatile, divorce can improve the situation. Often, stepparents and parental squabbles create trauma for children during divorce. It's common for children to feel unloved or insecure. There's a mark of additional trauma if a parent left, was unreliable or didn't continue a connection. A difficult relationship with a stepparent or stepsibling amplifies the impact of these events. Other relationships may leave unresolved energy. Romantic relationships of your own, especially in high school or early twenties, can be formative, especially if there were power imbalances in the relationship or a difficult breakup.

Bullying or discrimination. Bullying can happen at any age. School, home, neighborhood, workplace, military or community groups are just some places where bullying can happen. The definition of bullying from the Anti-Bullying Alliance is "The repetitive, intentional hurting of one person or group by another person or group where the relationship involves an imbalance of power. Bullying can be physical, verbal or psychological. It can happen face-to-face or online." This is a common situation that results in significant energy blockages. Include threatening bosses, discrimination and other abuses of power.

Death of a loved one. The passing of a loved one is a difficult life experience, amplified if you don't have the skills or support to fully process your emotions. Energetic blockages are likely in families that don't openly express feelings or frown on emotional expression. If you were unable to process the loss or the circumstances of the loss (for instance, in cases of medical error, suicide or a traumatic accident), there may be related energy blockages.

Feeling unsafe expressing yourself. When you feel unsafe to express how you really feel or act the way you wish, emotional energy can become stored. If you were the people pleaser who managed a volatile, domineering or controlling parent to keep the peace, your needs were likely suppressed. This type of situation often results in energy blockages and dysfunction in the energy centers that govern personal safety, personal power and self-expression.

Financial, food and shelter insecurity. Not having sufficient resources to meet physical needs creates dysfunction in the energy system. It also creates a deep sense of lack. Insufficiency affects how you view life for years to come unless you clear the energy blockages.

Lack is a mindset and a belief system, born of trauma that affects you in many ways. You may start to believe that if others are suffering, it's wrong for you to have plenty, you're not worthy of abundance or there will never be enough for you. Family history often plays an influential role (i.e., the Great Depression, wartime, crop failure). The mindset of lack doesn't have to be your future; clear the stored energy around lack experiences to begin nurturing abundance.

Household move. Moves can be exciting but also stressful. For children, moves can affect deep friendships and comforting routines, causing the child to feel ungrounded. If the move resulted in a school change or leaving behind a community of friends without enough support to grieve the loss, energetic blocks are likely. If financial hardship required a parent to leave the home for work, the impact increases. I find that moving to a new community creates the most energy blockages for children ages five to 18.

Illness. Severe, lengthy or recurrent chronic sickness including mental illness in yourself or a loved one are common energy blockage creators. Mononucleosis, chicken pox, pneumonia, tick-borne illness, the herpes family of viruses and others can lie dormant beneath the radar, distracting the immune system and depleting body energy.

Recurrent infections such as tonsillitis, ear infections, skin infections or strep infections cause physical and energetic blockages. Hospitalizations in young childhood are common sources of trauma, especially if parents were not permitted or able to stay with the child. Stomach aches are often a sign of anxiety in children.

Illnesses such as kidney infections, pancreatitis, cancer, surgery, benign tumors or more can create stored emotion and belief systems. Include stomachaches, anxiety or depression in yourself or others if they were difficult or regular experiences. Chances are, if you recall an illness from your childhood, it had enough emotional charge to be worthy of consideration. Include mental and physical illnesses of parents, especially if you had to assume adult responsibilities.

Violence in the home. Volatile parents who are quick to anger and difficult to predict, who create violence either through words or physical action, create energy blockage.

Clients often tell me, "I never knew what would happen when they came home." Witnessing or being involved in fights between siblings or parents (verbal or physical), being restrained, hurt by peers or adults, punitive punishment including spanking, withholding of food, being locked in closets or similar events all have one common thread: they make you feel unsafe and deeply affect your nervous system.

In this chapter, we've talked about core stressors and the typical events that create energy blockages. This list is not exhaustive, but I hope it helps you connect with memories, situations, and experiences that may keep your energy blocked. Awareness helps you explore experiences that still influence your health and assists you in preparing to let them leave. As you move through the healing session in the next chapter, you will invite the energy of those experiences to neutralize.

Chapter 10: The Interactive Healing Session

Let's jump in and move some energy! I'll walk you through the process every step of the way. With my guidance, you will identify where your energy feels blocked and allow it to move, leaving you feeling lighter. Honestly, it can be that easy.

While it may seem you're simply reading the words on this page, I assure you that as you read this interactive healing session, my energy will join yours and we will shift these balances together.

Think of my energy as a scaffold supporting you as I direct energy toward various places in your body. If this seems invasive or odd, it need not be. When you think of a loved one or send a prayer to a person in need, your focus brings a part of your energy to them. I'm simply extending this quantum principle with therapeutic intention. Remember, this connection is used only for the words on this page, only what you want to allow and only what is in your highest good for highest healing. Rest assured, you're in the driver's seat at all times and in full control of your energy.

As we move through different body systems, we will ask your body to make you aware of blockages that need your attention and to easily release energy blockages that are ready to leave. As you follow the process, you can use the tools we have covered—especially the open-to-receive process from chapter six and the EMOT process from chapter nine—as desired.

If any energy feels stuck to you, use the tools outlined in chapter nine. Remember, you can pause at any moment to let energy move within you, process a memory or use a tool in your self-healing skillset.

Expect *aha* moments as you proceed. You may suddenly remember a forgotten traumatic memory from fifth grade when everyone laughed at you or a teenage car accident you thought you were over. As the energy blockage resolves, you'll realize it impacted your energy system in a way you never fully appreciated. It's time to uncover the energy blocking the free flow of vitality in your body.

As you move through the list of typical energy blockage creators, there's a telltale clue to know if you have unresolved energy around a specific event. If you feel strong grief, sadness, anger, worry or fear when thinking of an event or a loved one, that's a sign the emotional energy isn't fully processed.

> **Fundamental principle:** Strong emotion about the past is a clue that unprocessed energy lies dormant.

What to Expect

It's important to note that energy healing is an iterative process and your system is always in full control. First, realize your body will clear what it's ready to move, without creating discomfort. Let your body and higher self choose the appropriate energy to move each time you journey through the session. This isn't something you need to manage consciously; it happens automatically.

Second, this session is intended to be used more than once. Each time you read through it, different energy will move in your body. By opening to allow the energy to move in whatever way is best, you will maximize the results. Third, remember your body and higher self are gatekeepers: you are completely protected and safe throughout the healing process because your body is in charge; at any time, it can decline healing that isn't in your highest and greatest good.

If you are particularly sensitive, perhaps an autistic child or a severely depleted and sensitive individual, we set a special intention that the session will phase in over the next two-to-seven days at a pace with no side effects for your sensitive system. Rest assured, I work with people like you every day and my work is gentle while remaining powerful.

Let your body lead the way to allow healing at the perfect pace for your unique needs. Remember, your body is in charge of this process. I am the facilitator.

Session Instructions

Read the words of the healing session. You may wish to have paper and a pencil available to take notes about anything that comes to mind. Impressions you receive, no matter how small, are relevant. Allow information to come to your conscious awareness without judgment.

Use this session as you see fit, by listening all in one sitting or in bite-sized pieces. This is your session! Pause momentarily if you feel called to do so; this gives your body and mind time to process or allow energy to shift. Allowing introspection will further your goals. Let your mind wander back to a memory if it pops into your awareness. What did you feel or experience at that time? Do you feel this past memory in your body now? If so, where? Connecting to these pieces of information will help you understand what energy is shifting and healing in the present.

If at any time you feel overwhelmed, stop and take a break. If the feeling passes, you can resume. If it doesn't, take a break to do the grounding exercise in chapter six. When you feel ready, resume the session. It's always fine to leave or stop in the middle if it feels necessary. It may feel beneficial to find time to read the session in its entirety.

Plan to give yourself time after the session to digest the energy and allow for shifts. Self-care is a powerful way to facilitate continued healing as your body processes the session. If possible, try to avoid stress for a few hours afterward.

A Word About Pronouns in the Session

In this session, I provide healing energy and direction for your conscious and subconscious mind by using focused energy balances. Your higher self is an active participant at all times during this process, as is mine. I, therefore, use the pronoun *we* to accurately represent the involvement of not just my energy contribution but also both our higher selves, my spiritual team of healers and yours as well. So, without further ado, let's begin.

The Session

We begin our session together by inviting you to arrive right here in this moment. Allow your focus to leave your busy mind. Thoughts and daily demands start to slow. For the next little bit, allow your to-do list to be placed on the back burner.

Take a couple of deep, centering breaths. Breathe deeply, feeling the breath fill your belly, then release the breath slowly and completely. Focus on another breath and with it, let your mind quiet. Connect deeply to your body. Move your focus from your head down into the throat, and down into the chest or belly. Feel a sense of quiet move through your system as you become present.

Read the following permission statement to open your system to allow change. If possible, read it out loud for an added boost. Hearing the words gives you more ownership of your thoughts. Alternatively, if you prefer, read it silently to yourself.

"I give permission for the energy that no longer serves me to leave my system now. I allow this process to happen easily and without side effects. I give permission for my body to shift and heal, knowing I am always in full control of this process. The negative charge of memories and experiences will leave my system, helping me feel lighter and freer. I am one hundred percent in control and safe throughout this process, as my higher self and body are active participants in this session. Only energy balances in my highest good and highest healing will come to me through this healing process."

Set an intention for your session, if desired. If there is a particular life area you wish to change or a particular health challenge, bring it to mind and ask that the session create movement for you. You need only bring it to mind now and then you can release your focus on it.

Stress Release

We begin our session together with the nervous system. Your nervous system truly governs your health. Stresses of all kinds cause this part of you to be either in safe rest-and-digest mode or danger fight-or-flight mode. Most of us spend considerable time each day in fight-or-flight mode.

It's okay to have moments of stress, but when the body is unable to downregulate and return to balance, your health begins to suffer. Important body functions don't fully function in this state; they need significant time in rest-and-digest mode to function in balance. So, let's downregulate your nervous system.

Imagine a bathtub full of stress that looks like water. Perhaps your bathtub is overflowing, perhaps it's half-full. Whatever the case, let's open the drain and allow the stress to drain away until the entire bathtub empties. As this happens, excess stress stored in your body drips down from the head, through the chest, belly, hips and down the legs into the ground.

Allow the ground to absorb all excess stress. See your cells releasing all stress chemicals. Adrenaline and cortisol levels lower and reset. Feel your body's muscles relax as tension leaves. Let your shoulders drop, your hips relax, your arms and legs drop into the chair or bed you're resting on. Give your body tissues permission to let stress drip out and fall away.

Your cardiovascular, muscular, digestive and immune systems hold significant amounts of stress. At this time, let these systems release excess stored stress. As you empty your stress bucket, room for resilience appears. Now, let's balance the neurotransmitters adrenaline and cortisol, allowing a deep body-chemistry reset. Finally, let's balance the entire stress axis and hormones that regulate your stress response.

It's time to repair places in your body that feed on stress, keeping it locked in your cells. We repair excess cell receptors that rely on stress chemicals and reorient them to feel-good chemicals instead. Let those places heal, balancing your body and giving it permission to feel calm, peaceful, and free of pain.

Finally, let's boost calming neurotransmitters in your body, including endorphins and serotonin. With this balance, we boost calming hormones and decrease stress hormones throughout your body and nervous system.

Now, let's balance any fear in your nervous system. Often, your accumulated past experiences leave energy blockages or belief systems of feeling unsafe. Think back to the common stressors list and recall a time when you felt unsafe. You don't need to relive any aspect of this experience; just bring to mind this situation or even this time in your life.

Many of us have experiences that anchor fear, big and small. The reality of the experience doesn't matter; what matters is how you felt. If you're not sure which one to choose, just let your body decide and think of a general experience.

Give permission for the energy of this experience to neutralize and with it, emotional connections, including terror, panic and any other type of fear. Refer to the emotional encyclopedia if you feel the need to give your emotion further description. Let's survey your body and allow tissues or systems to release this energy. Allow the intestines, stomach, heart, lymph, spleen, lungs, knees, hips, legs, ankles and feet to release any stored fear. Let's go into the muscles of the hips and legs, allowing fear and anxiety to clear from the many muscles there. Allow the right and left side of the body to balance.

Often one side will hold onto energy, causing excess tightness, while the other side compensates with excess flexibility. These patterns lead to postural imbalances and pain. Here we release stored energy at the root of these postural imbalances in your body's muscles, ligaments, cartilage and fascia.

Take a couple of deep breaths to fully process this balance. If desired, you may also stand and gently shake or move your spine to help promote movement at all levels in your body.

Spine

Your spine is a super-highway of nerve connections from the brain to all the tissues of the body. Many different stresses from your life experiences can hinder the flow of information through the vertebrae of the spine, eventually causing pain and degeneration.

It's time to optimize communication through your spine by removing any energy blockages. Recall a particular symptom in your body. Perhaps it's sciatic pain in your legs, pain in your lower back, tingling in your hands or arms, pain in your neck or shoulders, tight jaw muscles or postural imbalances (weak core muscles, tight hip or leg muscles, stooped shoulders).

Also recall accidents or injuries that might have affected your spine: car accidents, falls, birth trauma, scoliosis, sports or head injuries, surgeries or anything else that comes to your awareness. Long periods of repetitive stress or poor posture could be included here, such as a long health journey, feeding a baby or being a caregiver. Bring to awareness anything relevant and focus on the pain, symptom or time in your life. Again, there is no need to relive a past experience. Just connect to it by bringing it into your mind.

Now it's time to allow energy blockages to unwind from your spine, starting at the base of the head. We balance the connective tissue in your spine, both the discs separating vertebrae and all the ligaments and tendons of muscles of the spine, back, core, pelvis, hips, chest, neck, and shoulders. Allow the connective tissue (a common storage space for energy) to release disrupting energy it's holding from past experiences you recalled. We also shift energy blockages you may not remember or know about.

Next, we allow the fascia to unwind in these locations. The fascia can become constricted and hold energy, much like scar tissue. Allow the fascia to unwind as it releases tension patterns. Next, let's include the muscles, which can become unbalanced, much like the fascia.

Just as we did before in the stress-release balance, we invite the muscles to release energy blockages causing postural imbalances, constriction of nerves, and possible symptoms including pain or overly tight muscles with limited range of motion.

Let's balance the nerve tissue itself, optimizing the flow of nerve impulses through the spinal cord, the peripheral and sensory nerves, and supporting the ability of neurons to convey nerve impulses in order to communicate. Finally, the cerebrospinal fluid bathes the brain and spinal cord, providing protection, nutrition and detoxification. In this fluid, we clear energy blockages, including emotional energy, physical toxins, immune challenges or impaired movement. Allow this balance to complete throughout your nervous system, spine and body.

Immune System

Immune system disruptions can underlie chronic health symptoms.

The influential role of inflammation, chronic viruses, bacteria, parasites and more on your body's health is becoming more deeply understood. Many chronic symptoms are rooted in subclinical low-grade infections that don't show symptoms of active infection.

The Epstein-Barr and herpes viruses are examples. Once you've had an infection, these viruses remain latent in your body. Any sort of significant stress can prompt them to reactivate. Let's start by balancing the cells of your immune system. If you don't feel safe, either consciously or subconsciously, your body may be locked in inflammatory mode, creating imbalance.

Your nervous system and the peacekeeper cells of your immune system lower inflammation. Most of us could use a healthy boost in our peacekeepers. We balance the strains of your microbiome that promote peacekeeper activity and repair the innate and adaptive balance of your immune system to decrease inflammation. Let's also clear fear stored in your immune system, mucosal barriers of the digestive tract, respiratory tract and the solar plexus energy center (spleen, pancreas, liver, stomach and small intestine organs).

Fear is often bound with infectious agents, so let's balance it here by bringing awareness to your immune system. This includes parasites, viruses or bacteria that can anchor such energy in your body. When the mind-body connection clears, the infectious agent weakens and the immune system strengthens, bringing healing. We allow fear of any sort in your body to be released. Now, wherever fear was stored, we imprint safety and protection.

Your immune system is a dynamic intelligent force, powerfully trained by evolution to keep you safe. As you release energetic blocks, the immune system starts to remove stress that has been stalling your healing progress. Here, we repair informational faults preventing proper communication between immune cells and communication signals, thereby boosting efficiency and synchronization in the immune system. We also downregulate inflammation.

The immune system will shift when the body feels safer and the nervous system calms. Quieting inflammation inciters will boost anti-inflammatory signals and peacekeeper activity. As you bring awareness to below-the-radar infections or biotoxins, your immune system benefits as neutrophils, eosinophils, macrophages, natural killer cells and T-killers go to work. They are the front-line defense to keep you safe.

If your immune system is currently in inflammatory mode, we bring balance by calming reactiveness and decreasing inflammatory communicators. Finally, we imprint the body with power to keep you safe. If you've been on a long health journey or you have a scary health diagnosis, chronic disease or chronic pain, you may have lost faith in your body, feeling broken and unable to escape the mess you feel you're in.

Realize this is simply a story, a collection of thoughts. Your body is out of balance, but it's just blocked, not broken. Let's search for and clear subconscious belief systems suggesting that your body is unable to get well. Once blocking energy and beliefs leave, the right next steps will come to you. However, if you believe your body is broken, solutions can't come. So, take a moment to visualize yourself as healthy and well. Connect to feelings of happiness, freedom, joy and vitality.

If you are unable to visualize this in your mind, go to a past time when you felt well. Go back as far as you need to connect to the image of yourself feeling well, walking outside in brilliant sunshine, feeling happy, strong, light-hearted and carefree. Connect to those feelings; your body can heal and solutions can come. Your body can achieve health.

Here, we balance your body chemistry and mind to allow the image to manifest. Align your energy to your vision, connect to it and draw it to you. Hold this image in your energy, owning it as your future possibility. Use this mantra: *My body is strong and heals every day. I believe in my body's strength and innate ability. I believe in myself.*

Stomach and Intestines

Like the nervous system, the digestive system plays a pivotal role in your health. The gut-brain connection is proven and highly influential for many health conditions, from anxiety and depression to bowel disease and allergies. The gut microbiome is a diverse community of commensal bacteria, archaea and fungi, influencing health. In my practice, I often find threads of mind-body energy that influence the gut microbiome.

By working with energy, you can bring better balance to your microbiome. First, we balance the entire digestive tract, from the mouth, esophagus and stomach through the small and large intestines, and out of the body. There are microbes in all parts of the digestive tract. We hold these areas in awareness and focus on two in particular that often disrupt digestive system energy: the stomach and intestines.

The stomach has a mighty job of digesting food, as well as life experiences. The stomach is instrumental in pH balance for the digestive system. It has to be in top condition to properly digest your food and keep your energy levels humming.

If the stomach isn't acidic enough, downstream digestive processes won't respond normally. If there's too much acid, the lining can erode. If the upper sphincter doesn't close properly, acid can back up into the esophagus, causing symptoms.

The microbiome plays a significant role in stomach health. Overgrowth or poor balance of bacteria can cause problems. Diet and stress can agitate stomach energy. Let's balance the microbiome function for pH balance and pepsin production. Here, we calm overactive stomach energy in earth element, directing excess stomach energy to the spleen meridian, its partner and balancing energy flow between the two meridians. (Meridians are the energy highways found throughout the body where energy flows.)

We now release anxiety and fear from the stomach, common emotions stored here. The stomach often holds onto these two emotions generated from overactivity in the conscious mind. Many children have stomachaches as a symptom of anxiety; it's common to store fear and anxiety here if you lack the skills or support to work through difficult emotions. Let's go back to your childhood to clear times when you felt anxious and stored that energy in your stomach. Separation anxiety, bullying and fear of failure are common. Invite your stomach to release any other energy that is ready to leave.

An agitated stomach usually causes an agitated mind and an agitated mind can cause agitated stomach energy. If you feel you never get deep sleep because your mind is racing, eat a lighter dinner and see if you notice a change. This will help calm stomach energy. Now, we ask your stomach if there's an undigested ball of energy. The process of digestion includes breaking food down, turning it over, absorbing what is useful and letting the rest go.

Sometimes a big life event is difficult to understand and process. A health diagnosis, divorce, abuse, job loss, trauma and significant accident or injury all fit into this hard-to-process situation. Let your body and mind share life experiences you've previously struggled to understand. We balance the stomach to process, break down and assimilate those experiences to help it do its work.

Think of this energy as a clogged drain. With proper balance, we can open and move the clog by allowing energy blockages to shift. Finally, we release fear and anxiety from the stomach lining, muscle layers and the stomach's energy system by lightening energy and imprinting protection, safety, and smooth processing of life and food. Let all these energy shifts move through your stomach.

The intestines are the primary home to your gut microbiome. Species of microbes live in the small and large intestines. Microbiomes are sensitive to stress—this is proven in medical literature. We balance stress stored in the gut and its influence on the gut microbiome.

We all have cells that produce neurotransmitters and neurohormones in the gut. Did you know that 80% of serotonin is made in the gut? If you struggle to feel happy, your serotonin levels are likely low, in part due to your microbiome. If the microbiome causes your intestinal lining to become inflamed, this inflammation affects the function of these hormone producers, as well as the immune system.

So, we repair the microbiome, inviting better balance among all species that comprise this ecosystem, including bacteria, archaea, parasites, viruses and fungi. We decrease the strains that are too high in number and boost the strains that are deficient. In my experience, specific energy threads feed dysfunction in the microbiome. Guilt, fear, need for control, grief and unworthiness are common examples. Invite your body to expose energy blockages that have been sustaining microbiome imbalances in the intestines. Do you have a thread of family energy or an experience from your own life around these emotions? Physical toxins and infections also influence gut balance. You may or may not be consciously aware of imbalances; just allow anything to surface that is ready to heal.

One of the biggest balancing acts for maintaining your health is the interplay between control and surrender. Healthy control helps keep you accountable with the discipline to reach your goals. Too much control, usually caused by fear, causes constriction in energy flow and prevents positive movement in your body and life. Healthy balance allows forward movement without rigidity.

Most people need to learn to let go, allowing life to reveal the next step, while retaining the discipline to take aligned action. This is part of surrendering and embracing the flow of life, admittedly a hard balance. So, here we hold these two major themes with healthy movement, especially in the lungs and large intestines. By working with the breathing cycle and peristalsis, we invite smooth intestinal muscles to move in a free healthy balance. At the same time, we invite free movement of the breathing cycle, intercostal muscles, and the diaphragm, bringing oxygen throughout the body. Resistance is cleared to allow your entire energy system to embrace the shift.

Heart

The heart is the strongest energy field in your body, greatly influencing health and well-being. It commonly holds stress, resulting in symptoms such as heart palpitations, anxiety, panic attacks, irregular heartbeat, heart disease and inability to feel joy.

Even if you don't have any of these symptoms, the heart also controls the immune system. Let's start by holding your heart energy and surveying for damage. Many people have had difficulties with breakups, stress-provoking relationships, difficult losses, betraying friendships or destructive coworker relationships, just to name a few possibilities. These events can affect your heart energy.

Clear your mind and let your body focus on perfect energy to clear for you right now. When you return to this session, your body will choose different energy to focus on each time. So, let's release and repair past experiences from your heart energy. Whatever your body is ready to process, allow it to come into the session energy. Heart energy can be damaged by difficult experiences just like your physical body. There can be scrapes, bruises, cuts, scars and more.

Allow the injuries to heal, leaving your energy more whole and functioning with more efficiency and balance. We lift away negativity from the heart energy center, including anxiety, fear, bitterness, betrayal, rejection, abandonment, unworthiness, guilt, shame, sadness, and vulnerability. Allow and release any other emotions that come to you. This includes energy in body tissues, your mind (subconscious or conscious) and familial patterns.

Acknowledge you've survived through challenging life experiences and no longer need to carry the pain of the past. These experiences have served you. Release them, honor their service and all you've learned and acknowledge your desire for balance throughout your being.

Allow the session energy to balance and repair heart energy, bringing in highest energy vibrations of joy, love, well-being, protection, support and worthiness.

An important heart balance is nurturing yourself. If your heart energy is constricted and armored from past pain, unable to love itself, the heart and cardiovascular system can be constricted and diseased. We balance the ability to nurture and prioritize yourself.

Do you know how to be kind to yourself, to create space for your body to heal? Do you rest without guilt, supported and lovingly nurtured by yourself and others? Allow barriers to surface and release any blocks to believing yourself worthy of deep nurturing. Perhaps in childhood, only achievement was regarded as success in your family, and resting was not valued. Perhaps time off to replenish was seen as indulgence, idleness or laziness.

Examine your mind about your past to see where you learned that focusing on yourself was bad, selfish, inappropriate or hurtful to others. It's time to drop these erroneous beliefs; your health depends on your ability to put your needs first. Think of the oxygen mask on an airplane: you can't help others if you can't breathe yourself. So, we balance your heart's ability to nourish itself, especially the coronary arteries and the entire cardiovascular system.

Judgment and Self-Acceptance

Tempted to skip this part of the session? It's relatively painless, I promise and the benefits to your immune system, liver and lower back are vast. Your body will thank you.

When you judge, criticize or reject a part of yourself consciously or subconsciously, you create energy blockages and disconnect part of your body from the healthy flow of energy. Starting in young childhood, focus on your first five years, surveying for stored energy blockages created when you were corrected or judged.

This can happen in a minor way, such as, "That's not the proper way to hold your fork," or in a major way, such as, "Why can't you be more like your sister?" I invite you to open to receive guidance on patterns, people, thoughts you may hear in your mind rooted in criticism and judgment. Whose voice do you hear in your head when that happens? When in your early life did you feel this way?

If you don't remember, bring family stories to mind. As those memories surface, allow the energy of shame, guilt, inadequacy, unworthiness, grief or suffering to leave. Imagine yourself placing your younger self on your lap. Connect to how this youngster feels and tell them, "You are perfect just as you are; I love and accept you now and forever." Say it like you mean it! This allows that inner part of you to recognize and release those emotions, feeling deeply accepted by yourself, right now.

The liver, small and large intestines, heart, spleen, lumbar vertebrae, and lymph system commonly hold the above-mentioned emotions. We invite all of this to clear from your system along with any other tissue or system in your physical body that may still anchor energy you no longer need to carry. It's like a big heavy backpack weighing you down. If you feel this weight, take it off! Allow yourself to stop carrying this burden and allow its energy to fully shift.

Now, let's move forward to adolescence. Allow your body to share a time when you felt judged, criticized, inadequate, rejected or even attacked by adults around you. Those could be coaches, parents, family members, friends or romantic partners. During adolescence, it's common for judgment energy to arise. With an expanding social network, influential adults in your life and your first close social relationships may cause challenges as you forge your own identity. Squabbles, difficult teachers, disapproving family and conflicts within friend groups can all contribute to feelings of judgment, criticism and inadequacy. Open to allow your body to surface energy blockages for clearing.

While you may consider what others think of you, an equally important factor for your health is your relationship with yourself. Do you know that if you don't accept a part of yourself you cut off vitality in your body? Often, there are a lack of role models to demonstrate healthy self-love in your childhood. When I began my health journey, I didn't know how to nurture myself; learning how was key to my recovery. Indulging or having fun is not necessarily the same as nurturing. So, I invite your body to share how you can prioritize nurturing yourself to build energy reserves and create sustainable boundaries.

Here's a quick test: place your hand on your chest and say out loud, "I love you," and assess how it felt. Did you cringe or resist saying it aloud? Did it sound disconnected or empty? Your heart needs this reassurance to be strong and resilient.

Often, judgment and harsh criticism from yourself and others is held in the heart. Think of a critical person from your past: a parent, teacher, coach, sibling, boss, friend, grandparent, partner, or other. Whose voice do you hear in your head when you make a mistake? Criticism from others and resulting cords of connection must be healed and released in order for you to achieve freedom.

Ask your body to release connections to critical people in your past. Doing so releases heart pain: hurt, grief, suffering, sadness, unworthiness, shame, guilt and blame. Criticism creates wounds (weakness) in boundary energy. We repair and connect to your unique gifts, confidence and sense of self.

Repeat aloud, "I am perfect just as I am, in my own unique expression. I have unique gifts to share with the world." Let this affirmation sink in. Your differences are gifts, not something that needs to be changed. Accept who you are for your next step to appear. When you heal self-inflicted hurts of the past and judgment from others, you repair the heart and lungs, including pulmonary and cardiovascular circulation. We release any of this energy that is ready for healing in your heart, lungs, cardiovascular and lymphatic systems.

Too often love and compassion are directed outward, not inward, to nourish yourself. We allow energy to repair your relationship with yourself. Loving yourself is the first step to wholeness and acceptance from others.

Shoulders, Hips, Knee Joints

Joints are common stress locations. Joint health relies on flexibility—not just physically but also in life experiences. Here we balance your ability to be flexible with grace and ease, and bend with life's challenges.

If you're rigid when change happens in life, this brings tremendous stress to your entire system. If plans suddenly change, do you consider the entire day ruined and miserably return home? On the other hand, do you go with the flow and quickly find an alternate plan and still have fun?

Wherever you fall on that spectrum, think of a life area where you'd like to be more flexible—sleep, diet, work or relationships—anything that comes to mind. Survey your system. Invite rigid unyielding energy that prevents adaptability to come to awareness and release it.

At the end of the day, inflexibility boils down to fear of not being safe, loved, accepted or simply feeling good. You may think that's not you, but often you're not aware that you have those energies, often a result of subconscious programming in the first six to eight years of life. You can reprogram conscious or subconscious thought patterns. Let's balance the three major body joints and their common dysfunctions.

You may "carry the weight of the world on your shoulders," as the saying goes, and so does your energy! Where do you feel burdened or overly responsible for others' happiness? Do you have to do everything yourself to make sure it's done right? Did you feel responsible for maintaining peace in your family of origin?

Any of those beliefs and others like them, can create a tremendous burden resulting from early programming. Note these are just thoughts and not necessarily true. They may once have been true but are no longer. It's time to recognize that you have the power to neutralize controlling thoughts. Let's release the energy binding those thoughts so their influence releases.

Let's survey your system for the false belief that the needs of others are more important than yours. This belief can form from family dynamics, interrelationships, formative experiences and relationships in your life. Recognize the presence of these stories, where we release the energy binding them to you. Free from this blocking energy, you will be able to approach life as it comes to you, without the burden of over responsibility. We balance this energy in your shoulders and hips, including the joints themselves, as well as connected muscles, tendons, cartilage and fascia.

The hips are a common site of stored anger and resentment. The gallbladder meridian has great influence on the hip joint. The natural emotion of this meridian is anger and frustration. Survey your past and present experiences for situations that made you resentful. Look for threads of energy in your parents' relationship for clues of hidden anger or resentment. Parental, sibling and partner relationships are common areas that generate stored anger or resentment. Can you identify a family dynamic in your past that created the foundation for these emotions for you?

It's often easier to see those patterns in others, especially parent or sibling relationships. Notice patterns or people that come to mind. If nothing comes up, survey your own life for anger and frustration. If you don't ever feel those emotions, the problem might be suppressed emotion. It's human to feel frustrated on occasion. If you handle it with healthy balance, it passes quickly and prompts you to make needed change. (Anger is your sign that something needs to change.) We balance the energy of your hips to release any stored emotion, including the hip joints, the major stabilizer muscles of the pelvis and hips, connective tissues and fascia. We also balance the entire pathway of the gallbladder and urinary bladder meridians to release blocks affecting energy movement.

Fear is a common emotion that causes joint pain. You might have knee trouble if you're often "weak in the knees" from fear. Do you feel unsafe in your home, community or at work? These patterns, beliefs or emotions don't need to be conscious to influence your health.

Let's survey your system for the stored energy of fear. Here, we balance fear in the knees, kidney meridian, legs, adrenals and nervous system. In particular, let's clear subconscious programming from emotional processing centers in the brain influencing how you feel, view yourself and the environment around you. Allow fear and anger to clear from your body and mind.

Another main stress on the knee joints is forward leaning posture. In my experience, this is caused by shame, guilt or unworthiness. Emotions like these cause you to lean forward to protect the heart and chest, resulting in a body out of alignment and balance. When you lean forward, your knees support much of your body weight. Over time, this unbalanced posture leads to abnormal wear and pain in your knee and hip joints. On the other hand, if you stand straight with shoulders, hips, knees and feet aligned, your spine and hips support your weight and spread the load evenly through the legs, not squarely landing on the knees.

Check your posture in a mirror to see if postural imbalance applies to you. Your body can balance emotional energy and flush away programming from the past. This corrects abnormal tension patterns as stored energy releases from postural core muscles and along the spine. We now allow your body to release stored energy causing abnormal tension and imbalance in body postural muscles.

The Endocrine System and Hormone Balance

Your endocrine system rules the show! This important system

includes the following hormones: thyroid, adrenal, reproductive and metabolic hormones (think hunger hormones and insulin).

Whether you wake feeling rested or anxious, if you're ready to jam to your favorite tunes on the elliptical machine or if you can barely crawl out of bed, your endocrine system is the orchestrator of energy and mood, along with many other elements of your health and well-being.

People in the Western world tend to live stressful lifestyles. Let's start by balancing your cortisol and adrenaline levels to allow healthy balance. If your levels are too high, we bring them down. If your levels are too low, we bring them up. Hormones have a rhythm that varies throughout the day.

Your adrenal hormones can be too low at one time of the day and too high at another, creating imbalance. A common sign of low adrenal hormones is the afternoon slump. A sign of elevated levels could be feeling wired but tired and not being able to "turn off" to get to sleep. Let's balance the daily rhythm of cortisol in your body, focusing on any time during the day when you feel anxious or low on energy and focus.

We'll also balance the hypothalamus, the part of your brain that works with the pituitary to manage communication when the adrenal glands need hormonal adjustment. We also correct energetic disconnection to improve communication and regulation.

The B vitamins, magnesium and vitamin C are necessary nutrients depleted by stress. We balance your ability to absorb and efficiently use these nutrients from foods you already eat. Fruits and vegetables provide important necessary daily nutrition for your endocrine system. If you don't eat a colorful variety of foods, consider prioritizing your diet by expanding nutrition for robust health.

Your thyroid gland manages your energy levels. If you often feel tired and cold, consider having your hormone levels checked. The thyroid gland is located in your throat and from a psychospiritual standpoint, governs your ability to express yourself. If self-expression was suppressed in your childhood, your hormonal system could be affected.

Survey and identify past situations or people who made you afraid, who criticized or belittled you. This pain causes fear that interferes with your self-expression. You may hesitate to speak up or you may feel disempowered, thinking, "It won't do any good anyway."

Look into your past to see what comes up. Another aspect of expression is the ability to share emotions or even let them out. If in the past it wasn't safe to share how you felt or you weren't heard or felt you were rejected, this energy center can become blocked and heavy with suppressed emotion.

We balance your throat by pulling out suppressed energy blockages that are ready to be cleared. Also, let's detox the thyroid, which is sensitive to toxins in the environment. Heavy metals, halides (chlorine, bromine and more) and endocrine disruptors can all play a role in blocking the thyroid's ability to produce or use hormones. Here we focus energy to boost movement through your thyroid cells, releasing emotional and physical toxins at any level.

Let's balance your metabolic hormones and their relationship with energy levels. Your body cells use glucose for energy. Insulin shuttles sugar from your blood to the cells where it fuels the many functions of your body.

However, because of the excess added sugars and carbohydrates found in the standard American diet, your cells get tired of listening to insulin. The receptors become desensitized, stop hearing signals and require more and more insulin to carry out the same job. If the process isn't corrected, insulin resistance may develop. Blood sugar levels rise when the body can't keep up delivering glucose to cells.

Here, we improve the sensitivity of insulin receptors. This allows insulin to more easily move into the cells. The other major piece of the puzzle is insulin production, which manages sugar—the sweetness of life. By balancing the pancreas and the cells that produce insulin, you're able to boost adaptability and happiness.

If you can't feel joy or well-being, look for energy blockages that may be interfering. The sweetness of life is managed by the pancreas, where energy blockages can occur, often caused by fear and difficulty receiving. So, we clear fear of feeling unsafe or receiving abundance, fear that blocks wellbeing in the pancreas. This can originate from environmental energy inside your body or from someone in your life.

We allow your body to release this energy from the past, along with belief systems programmed through past experiences. This frees the pancreas to regulate blood sugar in a more balanced way.

Finally, another barrier to enjoying the sweetness of life is the idea of suffering. Belief systems about suffering run in families and cultures. Often, families show abundant love when one endures hardship, creating belief systems that receiving love requires suffering. We invite suffering to release from your body or mind, including the pancreas, and we invite the ability to enjoy the sweetness life brings to you. We imprint the following affirmation into your body now: "I'm worthy of enjoying the sweetness of life with ease and I welcome it now."

Connect to Your Innate Healing Ability

The last stop in this session focuses on your connection to your innate ability to heal. How does your body know how to heal, and where does that intelligence come from? If you suffer from chronic health symptoms or have family members with chronic health problems, you may not believe in your body's ability to heal. The conditioned thoughts of "My body is broken," or "This is irreversible," or "I'm beyond hope" loop in your head. As each new healing opportunity fails to help, better health feels more distant, you become demoralized, and those thoughts get stronger. But have hope: there is a way to stop this cycle!

First, let's disconnect you from false beliefs. Remember, thoughts are just stories; they may be true but they're just as easily false. Let's survey your subconscious mind for false beliefs about your body and health.

Your body is your partner: the only constant that's been with you since before birth and will be with you until your last breath. The body requires connection and the absence of love creates disconnection. When you reject your body because you feel it failed you, you create disconnection. When you start believing in your body, energy suddenly begins to shift and nourish the body.

Let's hold and clear energy of disconnection or lack of cooperation between your mind and body. As you allow energy to shift, make a commitment to always be an unwavering source of support for your body.

The body's innate intelligence guides healing on all levels but it can become disconnected. We repair the connection by allowing a smooth flow of information from the higher self to your body. The physical body relies on an energetic blueprint for proper function. I think of this as a recipe the body follows for proper function. If the recipe is disconnected, faulty or unavailable, proper function doesn't happen. So, we repair the connection to ensure smooth flow of information and energy, allowing your body to receive innate healing intelligence. Feel this renewed connection flowing in your body with ease to allow alignment, strength and balance.

Session Wrap Up

We've touched on many major body parts and functions in our session together. It's important to ground again after allowing energy to move in your body. Here, I connect and ground your energy to your body into your day-to-day life and into your surroundings.

Take a couple of deep breaths. Inhale, filling your chest with air. Hold for a moment, then gently let the air leave your body completely. Take a few more deep centering breaths, exhaling fully. Deep breath movement helps release residual energy. As you do this, imagine your focus coming into your body, connecting with the earth through your legs and feet. There is a grounding point on the bottom of your feet, and we balance it here.

This concludes our healing session.

❧

Revisit Self-Evaluation

Progress and healing can be measured in many ways. How you feel, your mood, resilience to stress, intensity or frequency of symptoms, and your outlook about the future are just a few metrics. Healing can be slow and steady, so gentle that you don't notice the improvements until you look back and consider where you started. Or it can be noticeable and significant.

Note: At the beginning of the book, you completed a self-evaluation found in Appendix A. Whether that was a day or two ago or a month or longer, the evaluation provides a way to gauge your progress. Now is a great time to revisit the self-evaluation and answer the questions to the best of your ability. It's important not to look at your previous answers to those questions until you complete the worksheet. Afterward, compare your answers to the previous results to see what changed through this process.

Chapter 11: The Everyday Action Plan

Information without an implementation plan will not yield results, so how do you take this information into everyday life to improve your health? You will always have challenging moments. Life will throw you challenging curve balls. With a few pointers, you can learn to navigate these moments with ease and grace and more importantly, leverage them for long-term healing.

Let's discuss strategies to implement what you've learned through this book, prevent new energy blockages and leverage everyday moments for continued healing. It's one hundred percent possible to have a healthy body and mind as you age!

Principles to Live By: Honor Your Emotions

It can be tempting to suppress unpleasant emotions, as it feels convenient and less painful in the short run. But that argument with your boss will leave an energetic residue, even if you feel it's been swept under the rug. It's imperative for your health that energy and emotion find a way to leave your body. Remember, current events often trigger past stored emotion, shining light on a part of you that remains hidden.

By allowing emotion to process, you release not only current feelings but you also clear past energy that resonates with it. By finding courage to allow difficult emotion to arise, you cleanse its energy from the past and present, making this simple process a potent healing tool.

Case History: Redirecting the Power of Mind and Energy

Kelly worked with a functional medicine practice trying to heal significant digestive symptoms. She was placed on a limited diet to eliminate possible allergens, according to a sensitivity test. After a few weeks, she was instructed to reintroduce foods to find the cause of her symptoms of diarrhea, cramping, anxiety and bloating. An unpleasant surprise occurred: each time she reintroduced foods she reacted to them.

Fifteen months later, Kelly seemed to be sensitive to everything she tried to add, with only a small number of "safe" foods remaining. Eating anything prepared by others was out of the question because of her significant sensitivities. She came to me in desperation, wanting to expand her diet. Unsure of what else to try, she turned to energy medicine.

We began healing the deep fear she felt when she ate, including concerns about food causing her pain and discomfort. There were also subconscious energy threads that traveled through her family heritage. That fear created thoughts, such as, "Food isn't safe," and "Food causes pain in my body," and "My body can't handle normal foods." This cycle created more fear of eating.

The failure of reintroducing foods piled on feelings of helplessness, brokenness and vulnerability. Her current food dysfunctions triggered more deeply-held fear below the surface, stored in her subconscious mind. We cleared fear from her digestive and nervous systems and introduced thoughts that food is safe and nourishing. On top of her food reactions, she also was experiencing fear because of the pandemic. Her job required her to report in-person and she worried about contracting Covid. We cleared her

122

feelings of not being safe during this time and during her years-long chronic health journey.

I guided her to notice when her thoughts focused on food being unsafe, instructing her to redirect her mind to, "Food is safe and nourishing." Within just a few weeks, she was reintroducing fresh foods to her diet with much joy and success. The suppressed fear around food dissipated. Eating became a safe and positive experience.

⁓

Years ago, my toddler was sick. His skin was hot as he rested in bed. His temperature was 102.5, right at the border of my comfort zone to allow fever to run its course untreated. The situation pushed my health anxiety button and soon I worried about how to make sure he was okay. Did he need to see a doctor and could this be a strep infection? Anxiety built and soon I realized I let my mind run away with fear and worry.

So, I interrupted my mind and demanded it to stop! I noticed that fear generated worry that didn't feel good. I reminded myself to keep a close eye on his fever and respond with action if needed. Just noticing and interrupting my gloom-and-doom thoughts worked and my anxiety lessened dramatically.

Since I'm aware of threads of worry in family energy, I took this a step further. I asked that all fear of illness from my family's past be released. (I later learned that a few generations back a child was lost to a typhoid infection.) I cleared fear-of-illness energy to free me from worry. My son's fever didn't spike further and by morning he was markedly improved. By noticing and interrupting those thoughts, my anxiety lessened and allowed stored subconscious fear in my family heritage to vanish.

Each evening, give yourself a few quiet moments to check in and process energy from the day. If you're not comfortable processing emotions with others present, do it when you're alone. If finding quiet time during the day is challenging for you, take a few moments to pause as you lie down to sleep. Explore how you feel and allow events from your day to come to mind and fully process them. Learn terms to describe emotion if you aren't yet proficient with this vocabulary. I didn't develop this skill in childhood; I learned it as an adult and you can too. It's much easier than learning to ride a bike, I promise. Consult the emotion list in Appendix C, an encyclopedia to expand your emotion vocabulary.

Be a role model to help others recognize how they feel and make it okay for emotions to surface, even unpleasant ones. Everyone is entitled to their emotions, even if their responses don't seem logical.

We all want life to be neat and tidy; but honestly, reality is messier than that. Live for yourself and those around you. All feelings are allowed but you must remain in control of your behavior. By working with emotion, rather than denying or suppressing, you allow a healthier mind and body for the long term.

Children in meltdown, siblings angry with each other and arguments between coworkers can resolve with discussion and recognition of feelings. This is far healthier than suppression. Be a thought leader to help others realize that emotions have energy and needs to move.

Honoring emotions does two important things: each time the emotional cycle is allowed and processed, it loses intensity and power. As you process a backlog of stored emotion, your initial reactions can be strong, scary or disarming. As you progress, triggering becomes less intense until it's just a momentary feeling. This is so much easier to handle for you and the people around you. Eventually, the backlog of suppressed emotion is gone, leaving you free for good.

Second, processing emotion prevents future energy blockages. What if you moved through life without storing anything? That's the objective and it's possible! Negative emotion is part of being human;

it can't be fully avoided but the way you cope with it can be so smooth and easy it doesn't feel negative at all. In this state, your body will be healthier, you'll be happier, age more gracefully and be more resilient. This is true health freedom.

Honor Your Energetic Boundaries

If you have compromised health, it's easy to put your needs last. In my practice, I find this is a major vulnerability that sets you up for chronic health problems. In fact, I'd say that in order to recover health, the pattern of putting yourself as the last priority has to be disrupted. Worrying about others, trying to keep the peace and staying safe are patterns that may have served and protected you in your past but now they hold you back from stepping into your empowered, healthy self. They must go!

We often erroneously believe that if we put our needs first, others' needs will not be met. But that's a false narrative. When you're rested and tended, you have more energy to give. This helps you meet others' needs authentically with more presence.

Dinner with an exhausted distracted mom is a far different experience than dinner with a rested and engaged mom who wants to hear how your day went. Energetically, the latter is a healthier environment for the entire family and it's only possible when your needs are met.

Protect your energy by learning to say no. Learn to make your family and yourself priorities. View your energy like a bank account that needs to rebuild an emergency fund. Say no to extra energy expenditures and become a fierce protector of your energy.

Minimize time with friends or family who drain your energy and maximize time with people who make you feel loved and rested. Don't volunteer if you can barely get off the couch; others can pick up the slack while you get much-needed rest. It's easy to feel guilty if you don't jump in to help. Focus on your number one priority when you feel unwell: your health and well-being. After you are well, you'll have opportunities to give to others in a balanced way that fills you rather than drains you.

After all, no one else will put you first, so you owe it to yourself to do so. Even enjoyable fun outings can drain your energy if you're actively working to recover your health. If a potential situation creates stress for you, just say no, guilt-free. Instead, spend your energy wisely with outings and companions that support, nourish and fulfill you.

Be Your Own Healthcare Advocate

To move through life with good health you must seize control of your healthcare. Gone are the days when you could trust your local family doctor to make the best choices for you. In our current medical care system, doctors focus on their specialties and often leave you, the patient, to advocate for yourself.

Most general practice physicians aren't trained in mental health, nutrition, stress and the myriad other factors that significantly affect health. There's a limit to what a doctor can do in a fifteen-minute appointment when major interventions need to be discussed. And so, you must play an active role in healthcare decisions that affect you.

You have one powerful secret weapon: you know your body. You know what helps it feel better and what doesn't. You have a gut sense of knowing when something feels right. No one else on the planet has the wisdom you have about your body. Use it to your advantage by taking charge of your health and advocating for yourself.

Look up alternatives. See what sounds promising. Read research articles or have someone explain them to you. Make sure research is accurately represented and not misquoted or misunderstood. Be an active participant to make the best decision for you.

It's easy to feel intimidated by doctors. After all, they're the experts with medical training. But they're human too. There are limitations to what they know and what they're allowed to talk about and present to you, the patient. Who has to live with the decisions you make? You do. So, make sure you're comfortable with the research and know all your options, including those your doctor may not present.

If you don't like the options presented and you're driven to find an alternate solution to your condition, keep looking. Get a second, third, or fourth opinion, whatever is required for you to feel comfortable with a chosen plan of action. A solution will appear. You may have to look hard, but you'll find something that will help you. There's more than just one way to heal.

Take Inspired Action

What feels right to you? Albert Einstein said, "The definition of insanity is doing the same thing over and over again, expecting different results." If you hope to recover your health or the health of a loved one, you must make changes and take action.

The tricky part is choosing a path of action. But here's the thing; you can always change direction, correct course or choose a different path. To get moving and conquer inertia is often the hardest part. Take some sort of action! One action will lead to another, which will lead to another. If your mindset becomes a daily evaluation of "How are things going?" and "What direction should I take today?" you will arrive at a destination. It's inevitable. But taking *no* action means *nothing* will change. I invite you to ask yourself what inspired action would help you move forward to find your next right step.

Keep in mind there's no need to see the entire path to your destination. Much like the yellow brick road, you only need to see the steps in front of you. It's nice to have goals along the way, for sure. But don't wait to begin until you see the destination—you may be waiting a long time. Much of life is a journey. Inspired action will illuminate your next step.

Stop Destructive Thoughts, Create Empowering Affirmations

We all have difficult moments or days when confidence slips. In those moments, the old stories in your mind take over and steer you off course. It's important to notice destructive thoughts in order to interrupt them. They don't help you feel better, and they don't help clear energy blockages. In fact, they generate negative emotions that make you feel worse. Those thoughts are destructive, like saboteurs.

As you become mindful, you will easily spot negative thoughts. Once you know they exist and you identify them, you can interrupt and kick them out of your mind. Become a vigilant negative thought spotter and distractor. Distract yourself with the next best thought you can muster. This is a process, not a one-time job that quickly changes your thought habits, so positivity becomes second nature. Within just a week or two, you will notice the results of your hard work.

There are tools to help program positive thoughts, in addition to stopping negative ones. This helps curtail negative thinking in a proactive way. You've likely heard of affirmations—statements that introduce positive thoughts in your mind. No, you don't have to believe affirmations for them to work; that's a common misconception. The affirmation needs only to be relevant and feel within the realm of possibility for you. Simply read the words each day.

To boost your results, write the words on your bathroom mirror or somewhere you will see them at least twice per day. When your subconscious mind sees the words, even if you don't consciously read them, you introduce a new thought pattern. This can be powerful! I've removed affirmations I thought were no longer relevant, only to discover they boosted my energy, prompting me to put them up again. Appendix B includes simple affirmations for you to get started. Be empowered to modify them for your own use, create your own or search for ones that feel good to you.

When You Fight Reality, You Suffer

Fighting reality is like banging your head against a wall. No matter how much you fight or complain, reality will still be the same until you make a change. I used to think the path to freedom involved focusing on the problem to fix it. *If I can just figure out what to heal in my body, my food sensitivities will heal,* my mind said. I've since learned this puts the focus squarely on what you don't want; therefore, you inadvertently make more of it.

In my experience, this thinking doesn't heal chronic symptoms. Instead, focus on what you want to align your energy with. Alignment will bring the desired outcome into your life. When something doesn't go your way, don't complain, throw up your hands, get angry and stew in misery. This is the definition of suffering: resisting what is.

When a challenging moment or situation comes your way, always ask, "What do I need to learn for this to resolve?" Newsflash: it's an inside job or it wouldn't be in your experience. There's something here for you to work on. That question immediately puts you back in the driver's seat and stops the flow of suffering. Instead, creativity and change become dominant feelings to guide you to a shift.

Accept what is and ask yourself what you need to learn. Be open to inspired action. This is the path to change and discovering the next right step for you. Whether it's relationships, work or health, this process works to curtail difficult moments and circumvent suffering. Ask yourself what you need to do to improve the situation.

Denial Doesn't Work

In studying the law of attraction, I've tried denying physical symptoms. My thinking went like this, "If I'm creating my entire experience and everything is energy, I can decide not to be sensitive to dairy and eat it anyway." Wrong answer. I've tried that multiple times, because I'm an eternal optimist! This path doesn't work for one simple reason: energy is stored in your body, blocking what you desire. Until you find a way to remove stuck energy and its sabotaging belief patterns and emotions, denial won't bring what you want.

However, once you move the energy blockages and repattern your thoughts, the symptoms magically disappear. I truly believe most health conditions are healable. But denial is not the path to get you there—healing is. Don't use denial if you want true lasting healing. Face the energy blockages in your body and mind to become authentically free to enjoy radiant health.

Stop Giving Power to Problems

I spent years trying to find the right solution to fix my health problems. I'm an engineer after all, a trained problem solver. I didn't realize that my approach inadvertently focused energy on my health problems. Remember, where you focus is where your energy goes; energy follows intention. My energy was focused on my health problems, rather than on being well. The solution was to recognize the symptoms rather than dwell on them and focus on living my life with as much joy as possible, while continuing my health journey. This task was difficult because I didn't feel well.

When your identity is bound with symptoms or a diagnosis, you bind it more. If you work to recover your health but spend hours a day in support groups talking about illness, I encourage you to curtail activities that may not be serving you—you are inadvertently focusing your energy on illness. Spend that time on activities that help you feel well: a gentle walk in the park, attending a family dinner or any other activity that diverts your attention away from your symptoms toward healthy living. This is not always easy, but it's imperative if you wish to stop fueling a focus on what is wrong with your health. Instead, focus on your desired state of feeling well.

Create a Daily Process to Maintain Healthy Energy

It doesn't have to be hard, costly or complicated to keep your energy healthy and avoid creating new energy blocks. The tips below can help you manage your energy during life's inevitable ups and downs. Simple practices allow energy to move through your system and take only a few minutes each day. The hardest part is remembering to make time in your schedule. Pick at least one of the following to start. For optimal energy health, incorporate two or more tips.

Meditation: Meditation is a simple practice of calming the mind and focusing on the body. Sit quietly and focus on your breath and body to release tension or select a guided relaxation meditation from the many free sources online. Find a simple one that works for you. Start with just five minutes; most people can make time for five minutes before sleep. Expand to fifteen minutes as you feel ready.

You will notice less stress, more resilience and a quieter mind. Keep it simple. Don't lie down to meditate; you'll invariably fall asleep. That said, meditation while lying down is a great strategy I use when I can't get back to sleep at night!

Gratitude journal: Keep paper or a notebook or journal by your bed. At the end of the day, reflect and write down three things you're thankful for. With practice, this will take less than two minutes to complete. Focusing on gratitude changes your neurochemistry. It also helps your brain default to positive thinking more easily. Within a few weeks of daily gratitude journaling you will likely notice gratitude throughout the day, boosting the feel-good chemicals in your brain.

"I'm amazing" journal: List three amazing things about you every day, big or small. My clients find this the hardest exercise, but the gains are worth it, I promise. Push through awkward feelings by focusing on the positives about yourself to diminish negative thinking and short circuit your inner critic. You can include something you said, did, thought, planned or even something you wisely chose not to do.

Grounding activity: Use the grounding activity from the *open to receive* process in chapter six to simply be present. If you're walking the dog, or at the playground with children, put your phone away and open to being fully present. Anything that gets your focus out of your mind and into the present moment helps you reconnect to your body.

Mindfulness activity: Make any day-to-day activity mindful by focusing on the present moment and keeping your mind quiet. Mindfulness while driving, exercising, eating or being with family are all great ways to grant space for energy to move, emotion to process or intuition to come to awareness. All it takes is a quiet mind and being physically present. Another way to be present is focusing on the five senses. Notice what you see, hear, taste, touch or smell to automatically divert attention away from the mind.

Take five: Five minutes of distraction-free downtime allows you to process anything you need to address. This is a blend of meditation, mindfulness and intention to allow processing space for agitation, anger, sadness or other emotions. It works wonders when you feel agitated or stressed but you're not sure why. Take just five minutes to sit quietly or walk without distraction.

These simple processes allow energy to move in your system to raise your vibration with positive thoughts and feelings to help negative thoughts and feelings move out. Incorporate two or three habits into your day for just two weeks and notice the difference. Greater peace and feeling better are worth the effort.

Empowerment When You Feel Bad

Everyday life isn't always smooth. There will be ups, downs and challenges. Your job is to navigate the twists and turns with as much grace as possible, leveraging each step for growth. With practice, the mountains of challenge become molehills. You move through them quickly and easily, without resistance. This is the goal.

So, how do you handle the ups and downs with grace? Here I provide practical ways to feel better, strengthening your resilience. These are self-help tools anyone can use without training. They are always available to you. This is a great first line of defense to cope with life's stressful moments.

Quick Ways to Shift Your Vibe

If you're agitated and don't know why, it's a sign of disconnected emotion that needs attention. You may be grumpy and irritable for no obvious reason and can't shake it off. When this occurs, take a five-minute time out. Sit quietly, put your phone down, tune into your body and notice what you feel. There might be a sensation, such as knots in your stomach or an emotion. Maybe you feel nothing but suddenly find yourself with tears in your eyes.

Allow any emotion that comes. Recognize, allow and give it permission to leave. Often, just five minutes of sitting brings whatever is ailing you to the surface. Once it moves, you'll feel lighter and more peaceful. If you can't move the feeling in five minutes, there may be resistance. Tell yourself it's safe to allow the emotion to leave. If it still feels stuck, try again later or seek professional assistance. Sometimes there are blocks that need professional help.

Get Out of the Mind and Into the Body: If your mind is flying at warp speed and you can't slow it down or your mind is focused elsewhere, it's time for a body-focused moment. Use this simple process to get centered.

Sit quietly, close your eyes, put one hand on your heart and one on your belly. Imagine a light just above your head. Visualize the light coming down into your head, neck and chest. Imagine it beneath your hand. Focus on it. Imagine you're the light, looking around and noticing what's in your heart.

Allow your mind to focus on sensations or impressions. If you start thinking, bring focus back to your hand. If this experience feels good, stay there for a couple of minutes. Have the light continue into the belly below your other hand. Keep your focused awareness beneath your hand, noticing sensations or impressions. Refocus if your mind strays and hold focus for a few minutes. You are now present and connected to your body.

Get grounded: If you feel swept away by anxiety, confusion, fear or overwhelm and can't get your mind to focus, you may need grounding. There are two ways to get grounded in the moment.

The first can be done anywhere, even on an airplane. Sit or stand with straight posture, close your eyes and breathe calmly. Visualize tree roots traveling down your legs into the ground to deeply connect to the earth. Feel a deep sense of connection, branching and spreading into the earth with stability. Focus on it for sixty seconds and hold as long as you like, though a minute is typically enough to get grounded.

For the second method, go outside and lean against a tree or just put your feet in the grass. Feel a sense of peace and calm to clear your mind and focus on your surroundings. Being in nature bathes you in healing energy and calms your nervous and endocrine systems.

Gratitude moment: Gratitude is easy to use anytime anywhere to shift your emotional state. Studies show that gratitude activates the same feel-good brain receptors as sugar! Practicing just six weeks of gratitude changes brain chemistry and thought patterns. While this sounds too good to be true, rest assured it isn't. The next time you feel negative, think of something you're grateful for and feel the emotion of gratitude immediately shift you into feeling better.

In order to enjoy the benefits of this powerful activity, focus on something in your immediate life to which you can easily connect to gratitude. Examples are being grateful for clean water and a warm home, a supportive friend, your vehicle, beautiful scenery around you or modern conveniences of power, plumbing and temperature control—all wonderful! While feeling gratitude, negative feelings evaporate.

Self-Help Resources for Energy Awareness

The previous tools are intended as triage to help you align when you feel off. Here are everyday activities you can do to boost resilience and get ahead of stress.

Lean into moments of joy: In your busy life you move so fast it's easy to forget to savor the good times. A beautiful sunset, snuggling with a pet or a child reaching to hold your hand are easy moments to miss if you don't slow down and savor them.

If you feel unworthy of joy, you subconsciously pull focus away from feel-good moments. You can change this destructive habit by simply leaning into moments of joy. Make yourself stop and focus on feel-good emotions for just 20-30 seconds; it doesn't take long to have a significant impact. Then get on with life. By stopping, noticing and allowing joy to be felt and acknowledged, you give the universe a green light to send more joy. It just takes a few times before you begin to automatically allow joy without focusing on it.

Shake up routines: It's easy to get stuck in day-to-day routines. Up to 90% of thoughts are habitual. Actions are routine, too. Routine is comforting but keeps you stuck in old patterns. Making a change and shaking up how you move through life can have tremendous power to disturb old thought patterns.

This is true not just in daily routine but also how your subconscious mind serves up thoughts. Although it may feel uncomfortable at first, with a few tries you'll find opportunities to embrace newness rather than shying away from change.

Take a new route to work, try a new restaurant or cook a new recipe. Add a new activity to your weekend or shake up your morning routine. Any change helps create change, making room to welcome the new energy you desire.

Small changes lead to a big impact. The detail you're changing may seem unimportant but nothing could be further from the truth. Small changes lead to new habits and skills.

Start small to increase your odds of success. Look for changes you already need to make. If you really want to start meditating but can't find time, start small! Just five minutes each night before bed is an amazing way to nurture this habit. Who doesn't have just five minutes? The small nature of the change helps avoid excuses. It's much easier to find five minutes to add a new habit instead of fifteen, which can feel overwhelming.

Start small with emotional processing. If you don't like to work with anger and you tend to suppress it, start with a small moment of frustration. Feel it, connect to it and allow it. Once you practice with something small, move on to something larger. Before you realize it, you'll be processing all emotion and lightening your body.

What emotion are you missing: Is there an emotion you never feel—anger, fear, sadness? I have many clients who assure me they never get angry, looking self-satisfied. My standard response is, "I hate to break it to you, but you have an anger problem."

Avoidance is tempting, no doubt about it. It's the easiest path, but not the most sustainable. You may be a master of suppressing difficult emotions.

Never feeling a particular emotion means it is likely suppressed. We're all human, so the full range of human emotions should be in your experience. This doesn't mean you have to feel explosive anger— certainly not! But it's normal to sometimes feel frustration and aggravation.

Be aware of emotions you rarely feel and survey yourself. Notice what comes up. Are you afraid of certain emotions? Are you trying to be different from a family member who always had an excess of that emotion? Are you afraid that if you start feeling it, this emotion will overpower you? Whatever the case, explore and find out what is blocking that emotion in your life.

Gratitude and self-love journals: Earlier we spoke about the power of gratitude. Daily journaling is a favorite activity to engrain this pattern of thinking. Each night before bed, list things you're grateful for that day. They can be big or small, simple or sophisticated. They can even be things you want to bring into life that don't exist yet. Then list three "I was awesome today" points in your journal. Examples could be "I woke and exercised," or "I ate a healthy lunch," or "I did a chore even though I didn't want to." Have fun with it.

The lists can be emotional or physical. The power lies in forcing yourself to look at your life in a way you're not used to doing. Many of us habitually criticize ourselves instead of looking at the positive. These exercises train your brain to look at life in a much more positive way.

Affirmations: Earlier in this chapter, we discussed the power of affirmations and how they align your energy to new possibilities. Find ones that speak to you and rotate them often. Every month, ask yourself if an affirmation is helpful or needs to be updated. Read the words or use the mirror method to boost your results. I find the mirror method works best because it circumvents my conscious mind. Refer to Appendix B for simple affirmations that could help you or make your own.

These seemingly small activities can revolutionize your life outlook. They reprogram your subconscious and conscious minds to align more fully with joy, safety, self-love and gratitude. Higher vibration thoughts and emotions attract more high-vibration events into your life. The result over time is profound. Suffering disappears and joy and freedom take root. Ease and peace will become dominant states of being. Implement just a couple of these activities and in a year you won't believe the different person you have become.

CONCLUSION

Throughout this journey, we have talked about ways to work with your body's energy system to remove blockages and improve health. We've introduced the body's energy system as something real and measured every day by doctors.

We covered ways to work with your energy field to uncover places where it may be hindered or blocked. Blockages you can't see have a big impact on health. They build with time and eventually impact your body, resulting in physical symptoms.

Remember, there is proven research that mind-body energy disruptors lead to chronic disease. But now you've learned a way to heal blockages, protect your body from illness and yes, to heal illness that currently exists.

If you only take one thing from this book, let it be this: your body has an innate ability to heal and if it isn't healing, that ability is blocked. There are ways to repair it using non-invasive, non-traumatic methods. This book is the tip of the iceberg of what is possible with energy medicine focused on healing your physical, mental and emotional body.

If this book speaks to you, don't stop here. Take the next step to recover your health and reclaim your life. You're worth it. No matter what the rest of the world says, people use energy medicine every day to heal from big scary illnesses that have "no solution." There will always be naysayers to groundbreaking work, but if you're struggling with health symptoms and you're desperate for a new perspective, I urge you to explore energy medicine. There really is nothing to lose. You were meant to experience a life of freedom and health. It is my wish that you find the perfect next step that leads you to a life of joy and well-being.

REFERENCES

1. Appleton, Jeremy. "The Gut-Brain Axis: Influence of Microbiota on Mood and Mental Health." *Integr Med* (Encinitas). 17,4 (2018): 28-32.

2. Yaribeygi, Habib. Panahi, Yunes. Sahraei, Hedayat. Johnston, Thomas. Sahebkar, Amirhossein. "The Impact of Stress on Body Function: A Review." *EXCLI J.* 16, (2017): 1057–1072.

3. Jain, Shamini. Hammerschlag, Richard. Mills, Paul. Cohen, Lorenzo. Kreiger, Richard. Vieten, Cassandra. Lutgendorf, Susan. "Clinical Studies of Biofield Therapies: Summary, Methodological Challenges, and Recommendations." Glob Adv Health Med. 4, Suppl (2015): 58–66.

4. Felitti, Anda, Norbenbert, et al. "Relationship of Childhood Abuse and Household Dysfunction to Many of the Leading Causes of Death in Adults," *American Journal of Preventative Medicine.* 14, 4 (1998): 245-258.

5. Kalmakis, Chandler. "Health Consequences of Adverse Childhood Experiences: A Systematic Review." *Journal of the American Association of Nurse Practitioners.* 27, 8 (2015): 457-465.

6. Boullier, Blair. "Adverse Childhood Experiences." *Pediatrics and Child Health.* 28, 3 (2018): 132-137.

7. Mariotti, Agnese. "New Insights Into the Molecular Mechanisms of Brain–Body Communication." *Future Sci OA.* 1, 3 (2015): FSO23.

8. Delongis, Folkman, Lazarus. "The Impact of Daily Stress on Health and Mood: Psychological and Social Resources as Mediators." *Journal of Personality and Social Psychology.* 54, 3 (1988): 486-495.

9. Littrell, Jill. "The Mind-Body Connection: Not Just a Theory Anymore." *Soc Work Health Care.* 46, 4 (2008):17-37.

10. Hay, Louise. "Heal Your Body: The Mental Causes for Physical Illness and the Metaphysical Way to Overcome Them." Hay House Inc., United States. 1982.

11. Purves, D. Augustine, GJ. Fitzpatrick, D. "Physiological Changes Associated with Emotion." *Neuroscience*, 2nd edition, National Library of Medicine. (2001).

12. online.uwa.edu "The Science of Emotion: Exploring the Basics of Emotional Psychology," 2019.

13. McTaggart, Lynne. "The Field: The Quest for the Secret Force of the Universe." Great Britain, Harper Collins Publishers. 2001.

14. Zander, Ollinger, Volz. "Intuition and Insight: Two Processes That Build on Each Other or Fundamentally Differ?" *Frontiers in Psychology*. 7, (2016):1395.

15. Roohi-Azizi M, Azimi L, Heysieattalab S, Aamidfar M. "Changes of the brain's bioelectrical activity in cognition, consciousness and some mental disorders." *Med J Islam Repub Iran*. (2017): 31:53. https://doi.org/10.14196/mjiri.31.53

16. Antonelli, Barbieri, Donelli. "Effects of Forest Bathing (Shinrin-yoku) on Levels of Cortisol as a Stress Biomarker: A Systemic Review and Meta-Analysis." Epub (2019).

17. Wang, Weiwei. Sun, Yan. Chen,Yong. Bu,Ya. Li,Gen. "Health Effects of Happiness in China." *Int J Environ Res Public Health*. 19, 11 (2022): 6686.

18. Rabin, B. Ganguli, R. Cunnick, J. Lysle, D. "The central nervous system—immune system relationship." *Clin Lab Med*. 8,2 (1988): 253-68.

Appendix A. Self-Evaluation

This evaluation helps identify how you feel right now. Take care to neither sugarcoat your current state nor to amplify pain beyond what is present at this moment. The results of this evaluation are for you and no one else.

When you complete this evaluation, don't look at prior evaluations. It's important to start fresh, without considering where you were previously or what you said last time. *After* you complete the form you can look back to compare.

Before answering the questions, take a few deep breaths to center yourself. Bring focus into your body; a hand on the heart and a hand on the belly can help connect to the body and quiet the mind. When you're ready, jump in.

Physical Body

1. List any areas of physical pain in your body. Include chronic aches, acute pain and transient pain that comes and goes.

   _____

   _____

2. For each pain area, rate the pain severity on a one-to-ten scale, with one being barely noticeable and ten being you need immediate medical attention to cope.

   _____

   _____

3. For each area of pain, rate its frequency on a one-to-ten scale, with one being infrequent or randomly-appearing and ten being constantly present.

_____

_____

Emotional Body

Primary emotion categories: anger, grief, sadness, fear, anxiety, worry, lack of joy, guilt, resentment, hopelessness, despair, unworthiness, distrust, insecurity and judgment.

1. Using these primary emotion categories, list any emotions you feel more than a few times per week. Add any emotions you often feel but aren't listed here.

_____

_____

2. For each emotion, rate the **severity** of the emotion on a scale of one to ten, with one a minor annoyance and ten your focus is completely dominated by the emotion.

_____

_____

3. For each emotion, rate the **frequency** of the emotion on a scale of one to ten, with one infrequent or randomly appearing and ten constantly present.

_____

_____

4. For each emotion, rate the **duration** of the emotion on a scale of one to ten, with one a few short moments and ten a week or longer at a time.

_____

_____

General Well-Being

1. Are you able to feel joy? Yes or no

2. Do you feel physically safe? Yes or no

3. Do you feel emotionally safe? Yes or no

4. Do you feel supported? Yes or no

5. Do you feel hopeful about the future? Yes or no

6. Do you feel changing your life circumstances is possible? Yes or no

To download a fillable version of this assessment, please visit:

thehiddenforcewithin.com

Appendix B. Affirmations

Self-love and Acceptance

I am special. I deserve (self) respect.

I don't need to be fixed. I need to be accepted.

I honor my imperfections. I honor my journey.

Embrace the negativity within you; it will bring healing.

I live my life my way for me.

Joy is my birthright.

Everything my intuition leads me to do moves me closer to vibrant health; I trust myself.

Happiness is not determined by the environment; it is birthed from within.

There is no way to judge past actions. We are all different people looking back through the lens of wisdom.

I am perfect just as I am, doing the best I can in each moment.

The world needs to hear my voice.

The world needs me.

My needs matter: they are just as important as anyone else's.

There are no mistakes, only learning opportunities.

I value myself; it's important to put my needs first.

I deserve to love myself always. I'm worthy of self-love and self-acceptance.

Empowerment and Confidence

I am ready to value my time and health. I put my needs first.

I have the power to make decisions for myself and my family.

I have the power to change my reality.

It is safe to be me. The world needs my gifts. My gifts are powerful and unique to me.

Now is the time to start living my life for me.

It's time for me to be me. The world is ready for me now.

Embrace Health

I am ready to create health.

I am radiant, healthy and strong.

I lovingly accept every part of me. I love and appreciate my physical body. We are a team.

I disconnect all attachments to the pain of my past. My body moves forward with strength and stability.

My body is perfect for me. I am grateful for its service to me in each and every moment.

I joyfully love and care for my body; it is my partner in life. We are strong together.

I create health for myself.

My body is strong. I have confidence it can keep me safe and move me forward.

I am worthy of radiant health on all levels.

I trust my body and my body trusts me.

I am grateful for my body that serves me in every moment. My body is strong and able to heal.

I am strong. My body gets stronger every day and is able to serve me.

I give permission to let go of my family's past; it is not mine to fix.

My cells welcome and embrace full vitality.

My body is in perfect harmony with my soul and ready for my next step.

Surrender and Allow

Life is a string of present moments. Don't miss this one. Be present in this moment.

I receive from the universe with openness and gratitude. Its supports and guides me forward on my life's journey.

My family members can change their life when they're ready.

I embrace all of life's experiences as stepping stones that move me forward every day.

In each moment, I do the best I can with the tools I have been given.

It is safe to be me.

Light will always triumph over darkness.

There are gifts within me that need to be recognized. I discover those gifts with ease.

I am ready to allow my life's journey to unfold.

By accepting where I am right now, I allow my "right now" reality to change.

For everything I judge as not good enough, there is a reason why it might be perfect for me. I am open to receiving this wisdom.

I accept every life situation that teaches me how to move forward.

Movement and Change

I am no longer the fixer. I deny that identity and step into abundance.

The universe loves action. What action will I take today?"

I let energy flow within my body with ease.

The past has served its purpose. Now it is time to step into a new future.

If I step back, others can step up to support me. I relinquish control. I allow support.

I'm ready to own my future. I embrace change.

Abundance

I need abundance to live my soul's mission.

I create all the resources I need to live my soul's mission.

Abundance benefits all those in my community and helps me make the world a better place.

I focus on what I want to create. I unleash my creative energy to create the reality I want. I take inspired action.

I am fully deserving of prosperity and abundance in all areas of my life.

I deserve to have it all: body, health, vitality, strength, joy.

Appendix C. Emotion Encyclopedia

Fear	Anger	Grief
Abandonment	Animosity	Abandonment
Agitation	Annoyance	Affliction
Anxiety	Antagonism	Anguish
Apprehension	Defensiveness	Bereavement
Aversion	Displeasure	Betrayal
Betrayal	Enraged	Bitter
Distress	Envy	Crushed
Doubt	Frustrated	Defensiveness
Dread	Fury	Dejection
Fainthearted	Hatred	Depression
Foreboding	Irritability	Despair
Fright	Irritation	Devastated
Frozen	Jealousy	Distress
Horror	Mad	Guilt
Insecurity	Outraged	Heartache
Panic	Rage	Heartbroken
Phobia	Resent	Melancholy
Revulsion	Seethe	Misery
Shock	Sore	Mourning
Suspicion	Stew	Pain
Terror	Tantrum	Rejection
Timid	Temper	Regret
Trembling	Violence	Remorse
Tremor		Shame
Trepidation		Sorrow
Unease		Suffering
Vulnerability		Tormented
		Wretchedness

Worry	Sadness	Joy
Afflict	Anguish	Bliss
Apprehension	Blues	Cheerfulness
Beset	Boredom	Delight
Bother	Dejection	Ecstasy
Concern	Depression	Elation
Distress	Desolation	Euphoria
Disturbance	Despondent	Exhilaration
Doubt	Discouraged	Exuberance
Fret	Disheartened	Exultation
Guilt	Downhearted	Gladness
Hurt	Failure	Gleefulness
Irritation	Forlornness	Gratification
Lack of control	Hopelessness	Happiness
Low self-esteem	Insecurity	Hopefulness
Misgiving	Joylessness	Intoxication
Mistrust	Lost	Joviality
Mull over	Love Unreceived	Jubilation
Nag	Melancholy	Lightheartedness
Plague	Misery	Optimism
Sigh	Moodiness	Satisfaction
Suffer	Mopes	
Torment	Pain	
Torture	Self-pity	
Uncertainty	Sorrow	
Uneasy	Unhappiness	
Woe	Unsupported	
	Wretchedness	

This list is adapted from an unknown source.

Download the Emotion Encyclopedia graphic at:
thehiddenforcewithin.com

Acknowledgments

Thank you to my trusted clients who reviewed this book and shared their insightful comments for improvement, including Kristi Parker, Rebecca Bender, Cindia Stewart and Jessica Haney. Your invaluable input helped me escape my practitioner brain and speak to the reader.

Thank you to my publishing team, including editors Barbara and Donna, who guided my words and corrected my grammar while tolerating my stream of comments, questions and suggestions.

I would like to thank each and every client who has stepped through my office doors, informing my work, teaching me wisdom through experience and showing me the body can miraculously heal.

Most of all, I would like to thank my husband, Roel Lascano, the most supportive and loving person I know. Without your unwavering support and grounding presence and "holding down the fort" during late-night writing sessions, I'd still have an unfinished manuscript. Your steadfast faith in my work is the wind within my sails, propelling me forward on cloudy days.

About the Author

Sarah Lascano is an internationally recognized healer, speaker, and author. After hearing the words "there is nothing we can do" during her own health journey and nearly losing hope, she became passionate about helping people realize healing is possible.

Sarah works with doctors and patients to bridge the gap between mind, body, and energy. She combines her medical experience and engineering training with expert healing to help people discover the root cause of their health issues to reclaim their health.

Sarah's healing practice and the RayZen Center for Wellness are in Stephens City, VA where she works with clients both remotely and in-person. Sarah lives with her family in Virginia. Visit her online at rayzenenergy.com.

Healing with Sarah: Beyond the Book

Sarah provides a variety of programs to support you in achieving your goals, whether you're new to energy healing or an experienced practitioner seeking to deepen your skills.

Private Healing

Sarah and her team of skilled healers offer intuitive energy healing to help restore your body's natural ability to heal. Experience powerful healing that integrates into your healthcare without side effects. Release past trauma gently—no need to discuss it. Strengthen your body from its foundation with healing that lasts. Book a consultation call with our healing team to explore whether energy medicine is the right path for you.

Events

Sarah hosts a variety of healing events, both virtual and in-person. These gatherings leverage the power of community to accelerate your growth in life, business, relationships and health. Learn transformative skills and tools, gain insight into navigating life's challenges and harness the power of community to heal.

Classes

Sarah believes everyone can work with their energy and heal. Her gift for simplifying complex processes into clear, actionable steps makes her classes both engaging and transformative. No prior experience is required.

Discover more about private healing, events and classes or book a call with the RayZen Energy team to get started at:

RAYZENENERGY.COM

www.ingramcontent.com/pod-product-compliance
Lightning Source LLC
LaVergne TN
LVHW051059080426
835508LV00019B/1965